TRANSFORMED!

The Power of God's Presence

TRANSFORMED!

The Power of God's Presence

by

Johnnie R. Jones

© 2010
Johnnie R. Jones
All Rights Reserved

Library of Congress Control Number:
2010920071

ISBN: 978-0-9825827-8-7

Previously published in two volumes: *Metamorphosis: Changes From Within* © 2002 (ISBN: 0-9719174-2-6; LCCN: 2002090708); and *Metamorphosis 2: The Transforming Power of Intimacy With God* © 2004 (ISBN: 0-976072-2-2; LCCN: 2004097453).
Revised - 2010

Scripture taken from the New King James Version.
Copyright © 1982 by Thomas Nelson, Inc.
Used by permission. All rights reserved.

S-Y-D Publications®
A publishing ministry of
His Abounding Grace Ministries, Inc.
McKinney, Texas
www.HisAboundingGrace.org

Printed in the USA by
Morris Publishing®
3212 E. Hwy. 30
Kearney, NE 68847
1.800.650.7888
www.morrispublishing.com

DEDICATION

To the One who has transformed me: Jesus Christ.

My Lord has revealed His dedication on a supreme level by mirroring His presence to me through the life of my wife, Diane. She is the epitome of heaven on earth, one who has given her life totally and sacrificially to her Lord and then to me. I would not have known the depth of sacrificial love had I not married her. Her life and her love for me cause me to give more glory to God.

I further dedicate this volume to my growing family:

Jenny and Shawn Martin, with

Amber, Kayti, Sarah, and Connor;

Tim and Marissa Jones, with

Rachel, Hannah, and Caleb.

It has been wonderful to see our family tree sprout its limbs.

PART ONE ~ THE WEDDING

CONTENTS

FOREWORD	*by Tim Jones*	7
INTRODUCTION		9
CHAPTER 1	*Don't Worry, Be Joyful*	13
CHAPTER 2	*No-Fault Assurance*	17
CHAPTER 3	*Brother Jesus, Father God*	21
CHAPTER 4	*I Come in Peace*	25
CHAPTER 5	*I Need Patience...Now!*	29
CHAPTER 6	*I Can Resist Anything…*	
	…Except Temptation	33
CHAPTER 7	*I'm in Love*	37
CHAPTER 8	*The Fruit is Ripe*	41
CHAPTER 9	*Transformed!*	45
CHAPTER 10	*The End is Near*	51
PART TWO ~ THE MARRIAGE		55

All Scripture is printed in **Arial Narrow, bold font.**
For the most part, all other **bold font** is added for emphasis.

FOREWORD ~ I ADMIRE MY DAD

Out of all the personal influences I admire or have admired, I, without question, admire my Dad, Johnnie R. Jones, the most. He looks like me 30 years from now. I don't think I believe it, but that's what people say. His hair is brown, overlaid with alternating strips of gray. We both have a double chin, his being slightly aged with a five o'clock shadow from time to time. We're roughly about the same height at 5 feet 10 inches. He's got me beat on weight though, by 20 or 30 pounds.

I think back when I was a teenager with my first car. I did not care to know or learn that much about automobiles or become a mechanic. My Dad, however, used to work on his car and lent me his knowledge to help me fix mine. Most of the time I can picture him halfway underneath my car, wearing a baseball cap, old T-shirt, faded work jeans frayed around the pockets and hems, and some old athletic shoes stained green from mowing, with oil and grease spots. In contrast with the above "Mr. Fix-It" attire, my Dad is best known as a pastor. He's a down-to-earth kind of guy. He's also funny, witty, and good with people. His personality could be described as fun loving and caring, but outspoken when necessary. He's someone satisfied with the basics in life. In public and in private, he displays a laid-back attitude. But behind the pulpit, touting the Bible with a perfectly sprayed hairdo, he transforms into a super preacher-teacher, reaching out to the unsaved, unpreached, and bringing back the disenfranchised. His voice raises several notches on the volume meter as he excitedly conveys confidence in his knowledge of the Word of God and the purpose of his sermon. Regardless of the topic, I always enjoy listening to whatever he preaches.

☙ Transformed! ☙

My Dad taught me that one of the most important things on this earth was people. This belief is truly reflected in his life. Any given week he can be found in hospitals, visiting the sick, and in people's homes. He also organizes mission trips and helps the needy with clothes and food.

Most Saturdays will find my Dad in a serene part of the house, studying for his next day's sermons. The quiet is usually only disturbed by the distinctive sound of the clearing of his throat. This indescribable sound is very unique; so unique, I have not been able to successfully imitate it even through much practice (reader should note that I consider myself a master imitator).

My Dad has taught me many things in life, most of which I'd attribute to visual lessons as opposed to verbal. I've learned by watching his actions and how he handles every situation he encounters. His unceasing happiness and contentment are reminders for me to focus on the more important things in life. Money is not the source of his happiness or contentment (did I mention he was a pastor?). He always puts God first in his life and he reaps the reward of doing so. What an example I have been blessed with all these years!

His successful, strong marriage is a loving example of the way marriages should be. It's a beautiful contrast to what I see on television or to divorces in other families. His willingness to work multiple jobs to provide for our family is another of his admirable traits. His determination to always make ends meet is a testament to his self-sacrifice for our family. When I think back to my childhood and my upbringing, I can remember many happy times for us when all we had was each other. That alone is a constant reminder of what life should be like. I hope I can be as good of an example to my children as my Dad has been for me.

—by Tim Jones, 3-28-01, age 23; written for a basic college English course. [Thanks, Tim, for such a neat paper. I love you, son, and hope you made a good grade on this paper. You get an A+ from me! —Dad]

INTRODUCTION

Change...they say it's the only thing constant in this world—except when you're standing in front of a vending machine. But in nearly every other situation, you and I must accept change. The world is changing and so are you. Hopefully, the changes around you are for the best. But sometimes—well, let's face it—many times things change in ways you didn't calculate.

You need to make a change, but—**ouch!**—change can be painful and a bit scary; like trying to find a new job, moving, losing weight, having a baby...**growing old!** So what changes are you going through that's got you thinking?

Some change is good. I remember, as a boy, fanning myself in a church service, longing for that oscillating fan attached to the wall to come back my way. Thank God for air conditioning! I also love the seasonal changes of each year and automobiles sure make traveling a lot easier. Okay, so you have to agree with me that some change is good—very good.

I'd like to tell you about another area of change that is desperately needed today. It's a change that, if you are willing to accept and apply, will transform your life. It's called a change of the heart—a change of your inner nature that expresses your attitude about people and about life in general.

The principles I reveal to you in ***Transformed!*** may help you avoid a serious illness or accident. I chuckled the other day when I heard a news report about a new dental disease called, commuter grind. It's the fracturing of teeth due to the stress people experience while commuting to and from work. The report spoke of a new mouthpiece that you can wear to protect your teeth while maneuvering in heavy traffic.

Transformed! is divided into two parts. In the chapters of **PART ONE**, I want to introduce you to the ultimate source of change. In fact, it is the most proven method of positive change ever written, tried, and achieved. This method has changed millions of lives down through the centuries and has withstood the test of time. When understood and applied, this method is the most effective because it affects the character traits of the person within you. Always remember, **change that lasts is a change from within.**

But is this method practical? Yes. Once you discover the source of this inner change you'll be amazed how easy and fulfilling change can be. I'm going to introduce to you how to change the most comprehensive basic traits of human nature. If applied, this method will change how you look, think, and act toward any decision that you need to make or any action that you need to take. And, best of all, it is backed by centuries of success stories from all walks of life.

As a guide, I will lead you through the bestselling book on change in the world: the Christian Bible. It is the world's number one bestseller because it focuses on changes from within. In the scientific world, some would call this type of inner change, a metamorphosis. Metamorphosis is generally defined as a change in form—thus, a **transformation.** In *Transformed!* I will describe the change process that takes place in a person's inner self. I will describe the basic inner character traits that can be transformed for a change that will last. Then, at the end of **PART ONE**, I explain how to make sure your transformation occurs genuinely from within. (Cf., **PART TWO, Introduction**, page 63.)

↪ Introduction ↩

Warning!
Mentioning the Christian Bible may send up a red flag for some; that's because there are diverse groups of people who carry Bibles who are anything but exemplary in the quality character traits I discuss. Unfortunately, there are some religious kooks out there who turn people off and away from the greatest resource for inner change found in the world. But, to use an old cliché, let's not throw out the baby with the bathwater. You must trust me that, after carefully reading each chapter, **PART ONE** will reveal to you the true source of inner change—a change that I call a genuine spiritual transformation.

To discover spiritual transformation, you must go beyond stereotyping and evaluate the biblical description of these great inner character traits. The genuine transformation that you will read in **PART ONE** will not target external or surface attitudes. I'm not trying to get you to turn over a new leaf in life. Rather, I will introduce you to a change in your inner self in order for you to discover a new life. To do this you must get beyond the typical "Christian" wrapper if you're going to discover the real ingredients that will bring genuine and lasting change.

Hotdogs
Ever bought a package of hotdogs? Product wrappers can be deceiving. The next time you visit a grocery store, read the labels of the ingredients of what we call a hotdog. There are hotdogs made up of turkey, chicken, pork, or something in between. Some of the ingredients sound pretty disgusting. Then there's the **all beef** hotdog. Now that's a genuine hotdog to me (just don't tell me what parts of the beef are used). And that's what I want you to discover in the following pages: **the genuine spiritual ingredients that will change you for the better**, from the inside out.

ಬ TRANSFORMED! ೞ

Slow Down

The process of spiritual transformation has nothing to do with speed. The key to the success of your inner change is to go slowly through each trait described. Each one builds upon the other. You must go slow enough to understand how to firmly release the power of transformation from within each trait in your daily habits of living. Once they are transformed, you will begin to experience a solid foundation of inner change. Think through each inner character trait with the precision of a brick mason or a surgeon. Listen carefully and read slowly all the verses listed from the Bible. Allow each word from each verse sink into your inner self until they have transformed your character traits from within. I'll explain how this occurs in the chapter entitled, **Transformed!** But first, let's look at the inner character traits.

CHAPTER 1 ~ Don't Worry, Be Joyful

You and I cannot stop change. Change will either make you bitter or better. The end result of your life will be in how well you adapt to change. If you want an end result that will produce positive effects for you and those who you will influence in the future, then read carefully the following pages in this book. First of all, take a Bible—any Christian Bible—and find the book of John. It's the fourth book in the New Testament section. I will quote from a Bible version called the *New King James Bible*. You can rely on this version or follow along in your own. They should be similar enough for each character trait to be discussed. Let's read about a character trait the Bible calls **joy**.

Jesus is quoted in John 15:9-11, saying:
> **As the Father loved Me, I also have loved you; abide in My love. If you keep My commandments, you will abide in My love, just as I have kept My Father's commandments and abide in His love. These things I have spoken to you, that My joy may remain in you, and that your joy may be full.**

Let's look at one more verse in the same setting:
> **Until now you have asked nothing in My name. Ask, and you will receive, that your joy may be full.** –John 16:24

Jesus of Nazareth is the founder of Christianity. In the above Bible verses, he is telling his followers that if they **abide in** his love, they will receive his joy to the fullest. He even taunts them to **ask...that your joy may be full.**

Being "**joy-full**" is a step in the right direction for inner change. It is a byproduct of inner love, another trait we'll discuss later. Joy is not the same as happy. Joy can be a direct result of happiness, but it's certainly not limited to happiness. Jesus said that in the world, you and I would experience pain and sorrow. But inner joy goes beyond physical discomforts or unhappiness. Everyone has times of pain and disappointment, and there are tears in real life. But as you continue reading, you will discover exactly what Jesus and others who wrote the Bible meant by genuine inner joy.

Three followers of Jesus, who penned his beliefs and practices in the Bible, were Paul, James, and Peter. Concerning the biblical understanding of joy, Paul wrote:

Now may the God of hope fill you with all joy and peace in believing, that you may abound in hope by the power of the Holy Spirit. –Romans 15:13

James says something similar:

My brethren, count it all joy when you fall into various trials. –James 1:2

Peter says,

[Jesus], **whom having not seen you love. Though now you do not see Him, yet believing, you rejoice with joy inexpressible and full of glory.** –1 Peter 1:8

These are the words of Jesus himself and three of his followers. They are telling those people believing him, that they are to be expressing **full** (or **all**) **joy**. There are many verses like the above I could choose for you to look at, but these should be enough for the point I am making.

Joy can mean happy, fun, peaceful, laughter, and/or contentment. Can it lead to change for the better? You bet! Joy is a character trait that is satisfying and relaxing. Joy is laughing or smiling instead of cursing or criticizing. Joy is tackling a problem or a decision with an attitude that there is something positive about to come out of this encounter. Have you ever watched an approaching storm with uncertainty? Joy is seeing the beneficial rain beyond the dark clouds of a storm.

ᛞ DON'T WORRY, BE JOYFUL ᛞ

May I illustrate? I remember an Alaskan fireman telling me that lightning strikes that cause brush fires are good for the ecological system. I thought this was an interesting statement coming from a fireman. He said the underbrush can get so thick that it starves the smaller plants that many creatures depend on for their food. Once a brush fire has done its damage, new plants begin to shoot up and before you know it there are all types of new wildlife flooding the burned area.

The above illustration is a reminder that what you may perceive to be a bad situation or encounter at one moment, could very easily have a positive application later on. It reminds me of a Bible verse that says,
> **Rejoice in the Lord always. Again I will say, rejoice!**
> –Philippians 4:4

Even when things are extremely bad and depressing? How can a person rejoice? Here's another verse that unlocks the secret to genuine joy regardless of the circumstance:
> **And we know that all things work together for good to those who love God...** –Romans 8:28

Now that verse doesn't say that all things that happen are good. But it does say that all things that happen can work out with a beneficial end. A joyful person is one who does not allow the circumstances to control him. Rather, he stays in control in the circumstances. A joyful heart does a body good. It's been medically stated that joy is a major remedy for many psychological and physical ailments. In other words, joyful people are healthy people.

Discovering and applying inner joy allows you to learn from your mistakes. You will keep your chin up and continue looking forward. Inner joy will allow you to see a silver lining in the approaching dark clouds of your life. Every approaching conflict, pain, or disappointment will become a new challenge for you to express the inner trait of joy—**genuine inner joy**! If you want to experience lasting change in yourself and your surroundings, start with an attitude immersed in what the Bible describes as inner joy. To do this you must be **transformed** by joy!

Additional Bible verses: (Note the character traits that refer to **joy**. I'll help you with the first one.)

Psalm 100:1-2 – **Make a <u>joyful shout</u> to the Lord, all you lands! Serve the Lord with <u>gladness</u>; Come before His presence with <u>singing</u>.**

John 17:13 – **...and these things I speak in the world, that they may have My joy fulfilled in themselves.**

2 Corinthians 9:7b – **...for God loves a cheerful giver.**

1 Thessalonians 2:19-20 – **For what is our hope, or joy, or crown of rejoicing? Is it not even you in the presence of our Lord Jesus Christ at His coming? For you are our glory and joy.**

1 Thessalonians 5:16 – **Rejoice always, pray without ceasing, in everything give thanks; for this is the will of God in Christ Jesus for you.**

Psalm 16:11 – **You will show me the path of life; in Your presence is fullness of joy; at your right hand are pleasures forevermore.**

Nehemiah 8:10b – **Do not sorrow, for the joy of the Lord is your strength.**

Romans 14:17 – **For the kingdom of God is not eating and drinking, but righteousness and peace and joy in the Holy Spirit.**

(Cf. Matthew 5:1-12)

CHAPTER 2 ~ No-Fault Assurance

"No fault" is a popular insurance phrase that was created to cover the expenditures of automobile accidents regardless of who's at fault. With no-fault insurance, both insurance companies can handle an accident without either party admitting guilt and without a ticket being issued for a violation, even though someone's at fault. This concept is similar concerning the "violation" against God that the Bible says everyone is guilty of performing:
> **For all have sinned and fall short of the glory of God.**

–Romans 3:23

> **For the wages of sin is death, but the gift of God is eternal life through Christ Jesus our Lord.** –Romans 6:23

The above verses teach you that, somewhere in history, man messed up his relationship with his Maker. This "accident" with God puts man at fault with him. To use a biblical term, man is a sinner. If the first half of Romans 6:23 was all there was to it, man would have no hope of having his fault with God dealt with. But the second half of the verse says that God provided a gift: **...but the gift of God is eternal life through Christ Jesus our Lord.**

This **gift** is experienced and received from God through an inner transformation provided by Jesus Christ. A spiritual transformation occurs when a person comes to God as a sinner and is forgiven by God of his sins. He or she is therefore not condemned by the announced judgments of God, which are to be administered at the end of the age against sin and sinners (cf.: 2 Corinthians 5:9-11; Revelation 20:11-15).

"No fault" does not mean you can get away with murder or any other illegal or immoral activity; there are normal repercussions and guilt associated with doing wrong. No-fault Christianity simply teaches that you will never have to pay the eternal price for the sin nature you inherited when you were born.

The Bible says,
> **There is therefore now no condemnation to those who are in Christ Jesus...** –Romans 8:1

Christianity's most popular verse of Scripture says,
> **For God so loved the world that He gave His only begotten Son, that whoever believes in Him should not perish but have everlasting life.** –John 3:16

Notice the very next verse says:
> **For God did not send His Son into the world to condemn the world, but that the world through Him might be saved.** –John 3:17

The above verses tell you that as one who applies this biblical gift of God's forgiveness, he or she will not face mankind's penalty for rejecting God's offer of "no fault." **No condemnation** is a label attached to **those who are in Christ Jesus** (Romans 8:1). The salvation act of God is to remove the fault of sin through a "once-for-all" death of a perfect sacrifice—the required punishment for mankind's sins (Hebrews 9:12). This was accomplished in the death of Jesus. One of the Bible words used for the result of the acceptance of this perfect sacrifice is **justified** (cf. Romans 5:1-2). God justifies a sinner and clears man's violation against Him through the blood sacrifice of Jesus Christ.

Now to get **in Christ Jesus** required the loss of blood from him. Jesus is thus recognized as the One who was placed on a first-century Roman cross and was crucified—sacrificed—for mankind's sin. The Bible states it several ways:
> **In Him we have redemption through His blood, the forgiveness of sins...** –Ephesians 1:7

ಆ No-Fault Assurance ೞ

Christ died for the ungodly. –Romans 5:6

But with His own blood He entered the Most Holy Place once for all, having obtained eternal redemption...and without shedding of blood there is no remission. –Hebrews 9:12, 22

The sacrifice of Jesus, God's uniquely born Son, satisfied the penalty for all sin for all time. This means you, **in Jesus**, stand in a **no-fault** position before God. This is your **assurance** from the Bible. It's like paying a fine for a traffic violation. Once the fine is paid, you are cleared of that violation. Jesus has paid the fine for your violation against God. When you go to God someday—and everyone will—He will **justify** (clear) your violation only through the blood-payment of Jesus. This sacrifice must be appropriated in your behalf. Keep reading the verses in this chapter until you fully understand this act performed by God on your behalf.

A person who lives with a guilt complex has no joy or peace. But wouldn't you agree that it's useless to feel guilty about a violation that has been paid for? In Christ, God has dropped all "search warrants" out on your name. You have been forgiven of your sins because his blood has paid the price. When Christ's blood is applied to your sin account, you are transformed from within and cleared of God's penalty.

Add this **no-fault** trait to **joy** and you have a person who is at peace on the inside as well as the outside. In fact, to know you are not to be condemned by God is a key element that leads to joy.

May I illustrate? When I experienced my inner transformation, I became one happy, joyful person inside and out. An inner burden was removed from my life. This brought peace and contentment to my life and allowed me to handle life's difficulties with a new inner attitude. When I got **in Jesus**, God applied His no-fault decision on my sin record and forgave me of my violations toward Him.

Now the above two inner traits of **joy** and **no fault** ought to make a thief want to turn in his work gloves. But wait! There's still more traits in this process to make your transformation complete. Keep reading and take note how each trait builds upon the next one.

Additional Bible verses: (Note the character traits that refer to **no fault**.)

> Romans 8:10-11 – **And if Christ is in you, the body is dead because of sin, but the Spirit is life because of righteousness. But if the Spirit of Him who raised Jesus from the dead dwells in you, He who raised Christ from the dead will also give life to your mortal bodies through His Spirit who dwells in you.**
>
> Colossians 1:21-22 – **And you, who once were alienated and enemies in your mind by wicked works, yet now He has reconciled in the body of His flesh through death, to present you holy, and blameless, and above reproach in His sight.**
>
> John 8:10b-11 – [Jesus] **said to her, "Woman, where are those accusers of yours? Has no one condemned you?" She said, "No one, Lord." And Jesus said to her, "Neither do I condemn you; go and sin no more."**
>
> Psalm 103:12 – **As far as the east is from the west, so far has He removed our transgressions from us.**
>
> Colossians 1:14 – **In whom we have redemption through His blood, the forgiveness of sins.**
>
> 1 John 1:9 – **If we confess our sins, He is faithful and just to forgive us our sins and to cleanse us from all unrighteousness.**

CHAPTER 3 ~ Brother Jesus, Father God

A third great asset of spiritual transformation is the family relationship you inherit in God. The Bible teaches that anyone who goes through this transformation becomes a member of God's current household; plus, he shares a new relationship with God and Jesus:

> **The Spirit Himself bears witness with our spirit that we are children of God, and if children, then heirs—heirs of God and joint heirs with Christ...** –Romans 8:16-17

Check this one out:

> **Now, therefore, you are no longer strangers and foreigners; but fellow citizens with the saints and members of the household of God.** –Ephesians 2:19

A fellow heir of God and a joint heir with Jesus mean you can have direct access to the unlimited resources of God. Can you imagine the potential of that? Think about it for a moment: the God who owns **the cattle on a thousand hills** (Psalm 50:10) wants you to have pleasure in and enjoy His resources:

> **Let them shout for joy and be glad, who favor my righteous cause; and let them say continually, "Let the Lord be magnified, who has pleasure in the prosperity of His servant."** –Psalm 35:27

Jesus calls his followers **brethren** and his God their God and his Father their Father (John 20:17). This statement occurred after his resurrection from the grave. In his new spiritual state of existence, Jesus was introducing a new relationship with his followers. You can be a brother or sister of Jesus:

> **For whoever does the will of My Father in heaven is My brother and sister and mother.** –Matthew 12:50

Spiritual transformation creates a new relationship with God and with Jesus. A person can actually have the Almighty God as his Father and Jesus Christ as his Brother. Not as a physical sibling, but a greater, satisfying spiritual relationship. What does this mean and what is the potential of change implied here?

You may recall from the last chapter that spiritual transformation places a person in Jesus. From this position a person now operates through Jesus. Notice the transition:

> **For through Him we both have access by one Spirit to the Father.** –Ephesians 2:18

Through Jesus Christ, a person can have **access to Father God**. The positive effects of this access mean much more than will be explained in this book. You can, however, understand enough to realize the potential you can have in life if you will trust God, as your Father, to do what's best for you and allow what's best for you.

When God takes over as your Father, He begins to work in you to shape you into His family likeness. He calls you into one body with other believers and with Himself. He continually works in your life to make you compatible with others and with Him.

As with any functional household, peace and harmony in the family depend on relational responsibilities. You can't just go out into the world and blow your family's inheritance without repercussions. Notice a responsibility here:

> **Therefore, as we have opportunity, let us do good to all, especially to those who are of the household of faith.**
> –Galatians 6:9

ಬು Brother Jesus, Father God ಜ

You enjoy the resources of God in the **household of faith** only as you apply the responsibilities contained in it. God and Jesus have set up their resources for anyone to tap into as long as that person has experienced spiritual transformation and use the resources for godly purposes:

And whatever you do, do it heartily, as to the Lord and not to men [selfishly], **knowing that from the Lord you will receive the reward of the inheritance; for you serve the Lord Christ. But he who does wrong will be repaid for what he has done, and there is no partiality.** –Colossians 3:23-25

Now let's try to put this into perspective. When a person gets into the family of God, they become a recipient of that family's inheritance. The resources of God's family are unlimited, as they are used for His purpose. It's like being adopted by a wealthy family. As you adjust and settle in, you begin to act differently because of your new surroundings and your new relationship in this family.

The Bible offers you **inner joy, no fault** with God, as well as a **new relationship** with God and Jesus. This new relationship comes with unlimited resources, within God's will, for you to enjoy life to its fullest. This is a promise from Jesus himself:

I have come that they may have life, and that they may have it more abundantly. –John 10:10b

The result of this new relationship is awesome. **In Jesus**, you can experience **joy** in any circumstance, **no fault** over your "violation" against God, and **access** to all His resources through a **new relationship**. But wait! There is still more to come in this biblical guide to personal spiritual transformation.

Additional Bible verses: (Note the character traits that refer to a **new relationship**.)

Philippians 3:20-21 – **For our citizenship is in heaven, from which we also eagerly wait for the Savior, the Lord Jesus Christ, who will transform our lowly body that it may be conformed to His glorious body, according to the** working by which He is able even to subdue all things to Himself.

Colossians 1:13 – **He has delivered us from the power of darkness and conveyed us into the kingdom of the Son of His love.**

1 Peter 1:3-4 – **Blessed be the God and Father of our Lord Jesus Christ, who according to His abundant mercy has begotten us again to a living hope through the resurrection of Jesus Christ from the dead, to an inheritance incorruptible and undefiled and that does not fade away, reserved in heaven for you.**

CHAPTER 4 ~ I Come in Peace

September 11, 2001—This date will go down in world history as the most devastating terrorist attack on American soil since its inception. This attack occurred while I was preparing the first edition of this book for publication. Terrorism is a stark reminder of the need for a most important character trait in civilization: **peace**.

Peace is what most people seek after. I believe it is the number one trait that allows mankind to dwell together in respectful harmony. Without some form of civil peace, man would eventually annihilate his kind. With this statement in mind, you have to wonder why there are so many wars still waging on? And why are many of them fought in the name of some religion?

In the book of James, we have an answer to this age-old question:

Where do wars and fights come from among you? Do they not come from your desires for pleasure that war in your members? You lust and do not have. You murder and covet and cannot obtain. You fight and war... (4:1-2)

These two verses alone pinpoint the cause of most wars: self-centered pleasures—a polite way of saying, greed. Greed is a destructive inner force that drives many beyond the satisfaction of who they are or what they may have. It says, "I want things my way or no way!" Yet that same passage continues to say that such self-centered pleasures will never satisfy:

☙ Transformed! ☙

You fight and war. Yet you do not have because you do not ask. You ask and do not receive, because you ask amiss, that you may spend it on your own pleasures. –James 4:2-3

Inner peace settles wars; it settles arguments and fulfills the inner drive for pleasure. It quells stubbornness and greed. Inner peace settles the heart; it dispels anger. Jesus offers a peace that he claims settles the inner turmoil of man:

Peace I leave with you, My peace I give to you; not as the world gives do I give to you. Let not your heart be troubled, neither let it be afraid. –John 14:27

A genuine peaceful attitude is offered by God and contributes to a healthy self-image. Having peace with God makes life much more enjoyable because it removes the fearful uncertainties of the future. Peace is living and acting in the assurance that God has everything in control.

And the peace of God, which passes all understanding, will guard your hearts and minds through Christ Jesus. –Philippians 4:7

Having an intimate relationship with God produces the peace of God in the inner self. This intimate peace relationship with God is only possible through a peace agreement with Him. Notice how peace fits in with the other traits in the following verses:

Therefore, having been justified [no fault] **by faith, we have peace with God through our Lord Jesus Christ, through whom also we have access by faith into this grace in which we stand** [new relationship]**, and rejoice in hope of the glory of God.** –Romans 5:1-2

And let the peace of God rule in your hearts, to which also you were called in one body [new relationship]**; and be thankful.** –Colossians 3:15

Do you see how all these traits begin to blend together? They compliment each other. In spiritual transformation, you cannot pick one trait and leave the other. This is the beauty of being in Jesus. When He transforms your inner self, His nature begins to dominate yours and you become peaceful. But how does it happen? Hang on;

ঞ I Come in Peace ☙

I will tell you later. But first, I want you to look at a few more inner character traits before you discover how **spiritual transformation** takes place.

Additional Bible verses: (Note the character traits that refer to **peace**.)

Ephesians 2:14a – **For He Himself is our peace...**

Philippians 4:8-9 – **Finally, brethren, whatever things are true, whatever things are noble, whatever things are just, whatever things are pure, whatever things are lovely, whatever things are of good report, if there is any virtue and if there is anything praiseworthy—meditate on these things. The things which you learned and received and heard and saw in me, these do, and the God of peace will be with you.**

Isaiah 26:3 – **You will keep him in perfect peace, whose mind is stayed on You.**

2 Corinthians 13:11b – **Be of good comfort, be of one mind, live in peace; and the God of love and peace will be with you.**

Transformed!

CHAPTER 5 ~ I Need Patience...Now!

"Lose 10 pounds in 10 days!"
"Be an instant winner!"
"Lunch in 10 minutes or it's FREE!"
"Why wait? Get your tax refund today!"
"Read this book in 30 minutes or less!"

We live in an "instant" society. We can order fast food on a credit card or know who is calling us on our telephones even before we answer the thing. We want instant access to the computer internet and the pages need to come up on our monitor screen as quickly as we engage the computer controls.

The same goes for our family life. Children have no time to play and/or interact with grownups. They are busy running from one activity to another. Kids are taught how to compete long before they are taught how to be courteous or polite to others.

Introducing the "Road Rage" generation. Yes, it's a new category of criminal investigation on our nation's highways. Many vehicular accidents, resulting in injuries and deaths, are now attributed to road rage. What is road rage? It is basically defined as the result of reckless driving by one or more vehicular drivers. It usually begins with an impatient driver cutting off another driver to get ahead of the other driver. The offended driver usually responds by catching up with the impatient driver and communicates his rage with the other. The exchange of rage many times ends up in an accident, fisticuffs, or even death.

"Mister Jones, would you hurry up and get to the point?!" Impatient? This is my point! Patience is losing its virtue in today's world. However, patience will do more to strengthen your inner self than any other character trait listed. How's that? Let me put it another way. Patience is to your character what a coat of sealing varnish is to a piece of fine furniture. Patience is to your character what a clear coat is to paint on a vehicle. It is that character coating that smoothes your relationship with others and makes you durable in any situation.

James says it best:
> **But let patience have its perfect work, that you may be perfect and complete, lacking nothing.** –James 1:4

Patience builds enduring character. Patience allows the root system of your character to develop, thus strengthening your ability to stand tall and bear a fruitful life. It is the ability to endure through the uncertainties of life.

In describing the many types of responses people would have toward His word, Jesus used a story of seed that was scattered on several types of soil. The seeds (people) that received his highest commendation were the ones that,
> **...having heard the word with a noble heart, keep it and bear fruit with patience.** –Luke 8:15

That phrase, **and bear fruit with patience**, is a primary key to understanding the entire process of inner personal transformation. As fruit takes time to ripen, so does the transformation of your inner character traits—**your spiritual fruit.**

Enduring patience is prerequisite for a fruit producer:
> **See how the farmer waits for the precious fruit of the earth, waiting patiently for it until it receives the early and latter rain. You also be patient. Establish your hearts.** –James 5:7-8

᛭ I Need Patience...Now! ☙

If you want significant inner character traits to develop, you must be engulfed in "clear-coat" biblical patience. And this comes only from the heart. There is a story of a man with an established heart and enduring patience. His name was Job and his lengthy story is found in the Hebrew Bible (Old Testament). The gist of the story is that Job lost all his possessions, his children, and his health. All he had left was his faith in God, an impatient wife, and a few friends. His wife encouraged him to curse God and die (Job 2:9). His closest of friends came along and spent countless hours talking to him, trying to reason with him that his problem had to be some secret sin that he had committed against God. If any man in biblical history ever had an excuse to break down and curse God and man, it was Job. But he held on to his belief in God and persevered. Because of Job's perseverance, God blessed him with more than he had at the beginning of the story.

God is called a God of patience:

Now may the God of patience and comfort grant you to be like-minded toward one another, according to Christ Jesus.
–Romans 15:5

Notice in this verse that what God is called, so man is told to be like-minded toward one another, just as Jesus Christ taught people to be. **By your patience possess your souls**, said Jesus (Luke 21:19). In his dialog with the churches in the book of Revelation, Jesus commends several of them for their patience, endurance, and perseverance (Rev. 2:2-3, 9-10, 19; 3:10). Patience develops endurance and endurance develops determination. This allows you to become focused in order to do whatever is necessary for personal inner transformation. Let patience have its place in your inner self and stop being in such a hurry. Stop demanding instant this and instant that. Don't get caught up in a road rage. In fact, stay at or below the posted speed limit and feel the difference of a calmer trip. Don't try to drive with the pack. Let them go on their hurried way.

Make decisions that will reduce stress levels in your daily activities. If your course load is getting you down at school, drop a few and find a part-time job that offers a service to people, like waiting tables at a local restaurant. If your job is killing you and your family life, first, ask for reduced hours. If that doesn't work, get a less stressful job and learn to live on less. Remember, the people who are always trying to keep up with the Joneses don't realize that the Joneses are always refinancing.

Additional Bible verses: (Note the character traits that refer to **patience**, **endurance**, and **perseverance**.)

> John 6:27— **Do not labor for the food which perishes, but for the food which endures to everlasting life, which the Son of Man will give you, because God the Father has set His seal on Him.**
>
> Romans 12:12— **...rejoicing in hope, patient in tribulation, continuing steadfastly in prayer;**
>
> Ephesians 4:1-3— **...walk worthy of the calling with which you were called, with all lowliness and gentleness, with longsuffering [patience], bearing with one another in love, endeavoring to keep the unity of the Spirit in the bond of peace.**
>
> Hebrews 10:35-36— **Therefore do not cast away your confidence, which has great reward. For you have need of endurance, so that after you have done the will of God, you may receive the promise:**

(Cf. Book of Job, James 5:11, 2 Peter 1:5-8)

CHAPTER 6 ~ I Can Resist Anything...
...Except Temptation

Self-control is not the same as being patient. Self-control is the byproduct of a disciplined character. A disciplined character is necessary for patient endurance and vice versa, but there is a difference. A patient person may have little or no control over a degrading or unhealthy personal habit, such as over-eating, pornography, gambling, or pride. These things, plus dozens more, can stifle the development of healthy inner character traits. Guilt associated with these vices can become devastating, destroying both a person's character and his relationship with others.

The Bible speaks of a great reward for those who endure temptations by self-control:

Blessed is the man who endures temptation; for when he has been approved, he will receive the crown of life which the Lord has promised to those who love Him. –James 1:12

The very next verses go on to say that God does not tempt anyone. He allows temptation to see if man will exercise self-control. The lack of self-control is expressed in the advancement of temptation. Temptation advances due to a man's **own desires** (James 1:14). Temptation that is not controlled or suppressed **gives birth to sin; and sin** [left uncontrolled], **brings forth death** (v. 15).

❧ Transformed! ☙

But why does God allow temptation? God, in His infinite wisdom, knew that it would be important to the development of man's inner character for man to be allowed to choose whether or not he would surrender to a temptation or exercise self-control. This allowance would make some temptations very strong and difficult to handle; yet man is given a choice.

Will God help in this matter? Here's an answer:

No temptation has overtaken you except such as is common to man; but God is faithful, who will not allow you to be tempted beyond what you are able, but with the temptation will also make the way of escape, that you may be able to bear it. –1 Corinthians 10:13

God's **way of escape** is through the power of that internal relationship we discussed in Chapter 3. His Spirit acts as a go-between to bring a convicting reminder in our thought process (cf. John 16:8). This means the power to overcome temptation is not from your resource alone. You have the resource of God's Holy Spirit to initiate self-control. It is the Holy Spirit who acts in your behalf to help you withstand temptation.

The Spirit is called a Helper:

And I [Jesus] will pray the Father, and He will give you another Helper, that He may abide with you forever—the Spirit of truth, ...but you know Him, for He dwells with you and will be in you. I will not leave you orphans; I will come to you. –John 14:16-18 (in part)

So you can resist the temptation to do things contrary to the biblical character traits explained in this book. You can initiate self-control and develop those inner character traits that will change you forever.

Do not be overcome by evil, but overcome evil with good.
–Romans 12:21

The solution is there before you. You can be an overcomer of any and all traits or habits that are contrary to the nature of God. All it takes is an application of self-control, added to the list of inner character traits, as you consider the process of spiritual transformation. You can do this because God loves you. It is He that

ঞ I Can Resist Anything...Except Temptation ca

offers you this aid by and through the Holy Spirit. His love will be transformed in you as you allow Him residence in your life. You'll understand more of this in the next chapter on love.

Additional Bible verses: (Note the character traits that refer to **self-control** and **temptation**.)

> Matthew 6:13a — **And do not lead us into temptation, but deliver us from the evil one...**
>
> Galatians 5:22a, 23 — **But the fruit of the Spirit is...gentleness, self-control. Against such there is no law** [limit].
>
> Hebrews 4:15 — **For we do not have a High Priest who cannot sympathize with our weaknesses, but was in all points tempted as we are, yet without sin.**

(Cf. James 1:12-20; 3:13-18; 2 Peter 1:5-8)

Transformed!

CHAPTER 7 ~ I'm in Love

Love is a word that has lost its foundational meaning. Some people confuse love with a certain emotion or feeling. But genuine love is not based on emotions or warm fuzzy feelings. It is founded on something greater and more enduring.
May I illustrate? What food do you really, really love? Mine's ice cream—I love ice cream! I can eat ice cream or frozen yogurt every day. (When I'm not dieting, I nearly do!) Now what if you **only** had your favorite food to eat every day, three times a day? I'm guessing that after a couple of days you will probably be thinking of some other food to fall in love with, right? Here's the point: If your love is based on satisfying an emotional or fleshly drive, it will soon become a dead passive feeling. Genuine love does have its feelings, but this is not its foundation.
Genuine love is founded on commitment. Ever read a wedding vow? A portion of it may say something like this: "I take thee to be my wedded husband (or, wife), to love and to cherish, in sickness and in health, in poverty and in wealth, till death do us part."
Paraphrased, it might say: "Honey, I'm committed to you for the long haul, regardless of what happens to our looks, personalities, health, or economics. I am committed to you until we both shrivel up like prunes and one of us bites the dust."
This is exactly how the Bible describes **real, genuine love:**

☙ TRANSFORMED! ☙

Love suffers long [is very patient] **and is kind; love does not envy; love does not parade itself** [not self-centered], **is not puffed up** [not conceited]; **does not behave rudely** [not obnoxious], **does not seek its own** [not self-gratifying], **is not provoked** [not hot-tempered], **thinks no evil** [does not get even]; **does not rejoice in iniquity** [does not lie], **but rejoices in the truth; bears all things, believes all things, hopes all things, endures all things. Love never fails.** –1 Corinthians 13:4-8a [author's explanations]

This kind of love comes only from a heart that is committed for the long haul.

During the trials of Jesus, one of His closest followers, Peter, denied knowing Him three times in one evening. About a week or two after Jesus' death, Peter went back to his fishing profession. One particular night, he and a few followers of Jesus were fishing and caught nothing. Jesus appeared on the shore the next morning, helped them catch a mess of fish, and they ate. While they ate, Jesus looked at Peter and said:

"[Peter], **do you love Me more than these?" He said to Him, "Yes, Lord; You know that I love You."** –John 21:15

Jesus asked this question three times, probably one for each of Peter's denials. After each of Peter's response, Jesus told him to help others. You see Jesus did not give up on Peter, even when Peter had given up on Jesus and on himself. This is true commitment; this is genuine love. The commitment in genuine love produces an inner trait that endures all things in every circumstance. Genuine inner love does produce feelings, but it is feelings like satisfaction and determination; feelings like challenge, courage, and compassion.

Until your love reaches the level that produces the qualities mentioned above, you haven't arrived at the level of genuine love that will change your inner self. Jesus says:

This is My commandment, that you love one another as I have loved you. Greater love has no one than this, than to lay down one's life for his friends. –John 15:12-13

ಱು I'M IN LOVE ಲ

This is the result of genuine inner love: a personal vision of the needs of others. It is the act of giving up your personal desires for the desires of those around you that you love or that need your love. The kind of inner love that causes change around you is only a dream if you do not determine within yourself to give up your life for the betterment of those around you. **Only as you experience inner spiritual transformation can you reach this level of love.** It does not matter who you are or your profession. You can reach this inner level of love as a schoolteacher, or as an auto mechanic, or as a sales rep, or in any profession. Regardless of who you are, where you're coming from, or what you are currently doing, genuine inner love can be transformed within you.

May I illustrate? My wife and I eat out regularly, usually during the weekend rush. The table attendants are very busy when we go. One night we were seated by an attendant who said, *"Hi. My name is Larry and I'm here to make your dining a great experience."* Although he was very busy, Larry checked on us regularly. He spoke highly of our order: *"You made a great selection!"* He incorporated his kids' love for his restaurant's food: *"They beg me all the time, 'Daddy, will you bring us some chips and dip home, please?'"*. When we asked for a carry out container, he brought us some extra tortillas for our leftovers and said, *"When you come back, please ask for Larry; I'll treat you right."*

You know what? I had a great dining experience. I felt good about giving Larry a generous tip and I will ask for him every time I go to that restaurant. He made our dining experience very pleasurable because he was committed to his job. My wife and I were his responsibility and his commitment level was extremely high. He convinced my wife and me that he loved his job. I cannot recall the name of another person who has waited my table recently, but I will remember Larry.

Do you see the difference? A self-centered life destroys a genuine love for something (a job?) or someone. It affects how you relate to those around you. **Redefining love as commitment** will provide an atmosphere for inner change like nothing else.

✼ Transformed! ✽

Additional Bible verses: (Note the character traits that refer to **love**.)

Ephesians 5:1-2 – **Therefore be imitators of God as dear children. And walk in love, as Christ also has loved us and given Himself for us, an offering and a sacrifice to God for a sweet-smelling aroma.**

Ephesians 6:23-24 – **Peace to the brethren, and love with faith, from God the Father and the Lord Jesus Christ. Grace be with all those who love our Lord Jesus Christ in sincerity. Amen.**

Philippians 1:9-11 – **And this I pray, that your love may abound still more and more in knowledge and all discernment, that you may approve the things that are excellent, that you may be sincere and without offense till the day of Christ, being filled with the fruits of righteousness which are by Jesus Christ, to the glory and praise of God.**

1 John 4:16 – **And we have known and believed the love that God has for us. God is love, and he who abides in love abides in God, and God in him.**

CHAPTER 8 ~ The Fruit is Ripe

The Spirit of God and of Jesus is the Holy Spirit. He resides in the heart and life of every person who experiences a spiritual transformation. Jesus once said:
> **And I will pray** [ask] **the Father, and He will give you another Helper, that He may abide with you forever—the Spirit of truth.** –John 14:16-17a

Notice the relational condition with this spiritual abiding:
> **If anyone loves Me, he will keep My word; and My Father will love him, and we will come to him and make our home with him.** –John 14:23

Jesus says if a person loves him, that person shows his love by keeping [obeying] his word. Then, in turn, the God of creation will love that person and both He and Jesus set up residence in that person's life. This is a win-win setup! The God who created you and loves you will set up residence in you as the Holy Spirit and begin to develop all the inner character traits in your life that we've discussed thus far. These inner traits are described in the Bible as fruit:
> **But the fruit of the Spirit is love, joy, peace, longsuffering** [patience], **kindness, goodness, faithfulness, gentleness, self-control. Against such there is no law** [limit].
> –Galatians 5:22-23

Love, joy, and **peace**—do these sound familiar? The **fruit of the Spirit** are those character traits that you have read in the previous

41

chapters. These are they that transform your inner self to give you genuine changes from within. The Spirit of God, in residence, works in you continually to replace the former worldly characteristics.

Worldly characteristics are degrading and harmful and are listed in the same Bible chapter as the above-mentioned fruit:

Now the works of the flesh are evident, which are: adultery, fornication, uncleanness, lewdness, idolatry, sorcery, hatred, contentions, jealousies, outbursts of wrath, selfish ambitions, dissentions, heresies, envy, murders, drunkenness, revelries, and the like; of which I tell you beforehand, just as I told you in time past, that those who practice such things will not inherit the kingdom of God.
–Galatians 5:19-21

If the Spirit of God resides in you, He will convict you of the wrong kind of fruit in your life. Once He gets **in you**, He will begin to help you drive this destructive fruit out of your life in order to fill you and transform you with the Spirit's fruit.

This is how the transformation continues to improve your inner self. This is why a Christian—**a genuine Christian**—has a great outlook on life and is a joy to be around. A real Christian ought to be modeling all these character traits—the fruit of the Spirit—on a consistent basis. Though not perfect, a Christian is always striving to represent his new family likeness:

For you were bought at a price; therefore glorify God in your body and in your spirit, which are God's. –1 Corinthians 6:20

As God's purchased possession, a Christian is under a spiritual influence. The Spirit is given to those who experience inner spiritual transformation to reveal the truth in all spiritual matters. His primary responsibility is to reveal the true nature of God to all mankind. Some people will accept and follow His revelation; others will reject it. Those who apply these basic qualities into their own life will soon discover an improvement that far exceeds any other remedy that man has to offer. The fruit of the Spirit will continue to

ೂ THE FRUIT IS RIPE ೦ಽ

ripen in a person's life and he will be a joy to be around in every circumstance in life.

Sound good? Want some of this? The next chapter explains how transformation occurs in your inner self. It will explain the moving from where you are now to where you can be, if you want the above inner traits of God's Spirit to transform your life.

Additional Bible verses: (Note the character traits that refer to a **new fruit-producing life**.)

> Romans 6:8-11 – **Now if we died with Christ, we believe that we shall also live with Him, knowing that Christ, having been raised from the dead, dies no more. Death no longer has dominion over Him. For the death that He died, He died to sin once for all; but the life that He lives, He lives to God. Likewise you also, reckon yourselves to be dead indeed to sin, but alive to God in Christ Jesus our Lord.**

> 2 Corinthians 5:1-2, 5 – **For we know that if our earthly house, this tent, is destroyed, we have a building from God, a house not made with hands, eternal in the heavens. For in this we groan, earnestly desiring to be clothed with our habitation which is from heaven...Now He who has prepared us for this very thing is God, who also has given us the Spirit as a guarantee.**

> Philippians 2:14-16 – **Do all things without complaining and disputing, that you may become blameless and harmless, children of God without fault in the midst of a crooked and perverse generation, among whom you shine as lights in the world, holding fast the word of life, so that I may rejoice in the day of Christ that I have not run in vain or labored in vain.**

John 15:4-5 – **Abide in Me, and I in you. As the branch cannot bear fruit of itself, unless it abides in the vine, neither can you, unless you abide in Me. I am the vine, you are the branches. He who abides in Me, and I in him, bears much fruit; for without Me you can do nothing.**

Psalm 1:1-3 – **Blessed is the man who walks not in the counsel of the ungodly, nor stands in the path of sinners, nor sits in the seat of the scornful; but his delight is in the law of the Lord, and in His law he meditates day and night. He shall be like a tree planted by the rivers of water, that brings forth its fruit in its season, whose leaf also shall not wither; and whatever he does shall prosper.**

CHAPTER 9 ~ Transformed!

The caterpillar senses an inner need for change as it prepares for its personal transformation. From within, the transformation begins as the caterpillar takes from its own resource and begins to weave itself into a cocoon. The cocoon protects the caterpillar from external influences as the transformation takes place. This inner transformation creates the external changes, but the external changes occur only as a result of the creature's willingness to submit to the forces from within. At the right amount of time, the caterpillar bursts forth from its cocoon as a remarkable new creature of beauty and grace—**Transformed** into a new creation!

The inner character traits you have read about are the results of an inner personal transformation. The ability to enter into the process of genuine transformation is not from a self-imposed source that allows you to change your mind about how you should act. No, this process can only occur as you willingly submit yourself to an inner source of change.

To acquire the above-mentioned transformation in your inner self requires a little reprogramming of the mind, will, and spirit. The experience is explained in another Bible passage. Read it slowly and carefully:

ಐ Transformed! ಐ

I beseech you therefore, brethren, by the mercies of God, that you present your bodies [i.e., who you are] **a living sacrifice, holy, acceptable to God, which is your reasonable service. And do not be conformed to this world, but be transformed* by the renewing of the mind, that you may prove what is that good and acceptable and perfect will of God.** –Romans 12:1-2

Paraphrased, it might read like this:

"I strongly urge you therefore, my friend, by the enriching nature of God, that you present your life to Him in complete surrender, holy, acceptable to Him, which is required of a servant of God. And do not mirror the external traits of the world, but be **spiritually transformed*** by the renewing of your inner being, that you may live out what is the good and acceptable and perfect demonstration of God's nature and will for you."

Anyone who has had the opportunity to watch a caterpillar weave itself into a cocoon undoubtedly has been amazed at the process. That caterpillar is enclosing itself into a self-made tomb! This entombment causes the caterpillar's body to transform—metamorphose—into a winged butterfly. This same caterpillar that had to inch its way along the ground or a tree can now lift itself up on the currents of the air and fly for the rest of its life. What an amazing change! What a demonstration of **transformation**!

Just as the caterpillar submits itself to the transformation, so you also must be willing to submit yourself to the only One who has written the book on inner human transformation. The initial act is accurately termed in the Bible as being born again:

...unless one is born again, he cannot see the kingdom of God...That which is born of the flesh is flesh, and that which is born of the Spirit is spirit. Do not marvel that I said to you, "You must be born again." –Jesus, in John 3:3, 6-7

---

* *Metamorphoō* is the first-century Greek word used for **transformed**. It is also the word used for Jesus when He was **transfigured** (Matt. 17:2). Therefore, it means more than just being emotionally touched or inspired. More on this in Part Two of this book.

ಬು TRANSFORMED! ಲ

Similar to the transformation of the caterpillar, the human transformation is like a dying process—not physically, but a dying to your limited, inner self-control. It is yielding your inner being and life to the authority of another. The Bible says,

If anyone is in Christ, he is a new creation [transformed]; **old things have passed away; behold all things have become new.** –2 Corinthians 5:17

For you died [when one is born again—transformed], **and your life is** [now] **hidden** [secured] **with Christ in God.** –Colossians 3:3

This is the apex of inner transformation. The spiritual event takes place only when there is a release of your inner self-control into the control of another. It's like a skydiver, up in the air, **ten feet outside the airplane!** It's wrapped around two interchangeable words, **believe** and **faith**.

For a spiritual transformation to take place inside you, you must first believe that it can happen. If you believe that it can happen, then you must release yourself into Him by faith. Faith believes that there is a living God, a living Jesus, and a living Holy Spirit who come to live inside of you:

But without faith it is impossible to please Him, for he who comes to God must believe that He is, and that He is a rewarder of those who diligently seek Him. –Hebrews 11:6 (emphasis added)

Faith believes God can change you and wants to change you. This has already been confirmed in the above chapters. You must now believe it and act upon it. Do you want lasting change? If you do, then you must follow through in this process of spiritual transformation. **It is essential; it is genuine Christianity.**

The process requires several steps. The first step is acknowledging the need. This is known as confession (cf. Romans 10:9-10, below). You are confessing to yourself and to God that you are following and are, therefore, controlled by the worldly character traits with which you were born (as previously mentioned in Galatians 5:19-21). This confession is an admission of being a sinner by nature, outside of God's inner possession. The Bible explains a sinner's position as an enemy of God and is due His eternal wrath. Why? Because mankind broke God's commands that established a relationship with Him. God's judgment for sin is a just response from His holy nature. Therefore, a sinner must stop, admit he is a sinner, and surrender himself to God.

Intertwined in this admission is what the Bible calls repentance. To stop and surrender to God involves an act of turning away from a judgmental predicament and turning to a new offer of salvation from that judgment. It is turning from a sin-dominated lifestyle to a Spirit-dominated lifestyle. It is turning away from a lifestyle that is contrary to the fruit of the Spirit (Gal. 5:22-23):

Repent therefore and be converted, that your sins may be blotted out, so that times of refreshing may come from the presence of the Lord. –Acts 3:19

Repentance is turning away from your self-control and turning to God, thus allowing God's Spirit to come into your life and change you from within your "cocoon." Sorry, the transformation does not take place outside the cocoon. God must first change you from the inside out before He can control your inner self. You must surrender yourself to the life-changing power of God.

The Lord is not slack concerning His promise, as some count slackness, but is longsuffering toward us, not willing that anyone should perish but that all should come to repentance. –2 Peter 3:9

This verse explains that God's part is complete; He is patiently **willing** and waiting. Now how long will you hold him off?

How do you surrender to God? You simply yield yourself to His authority. You stop being His enemy and surrender to Him on His terms. Your admission, surrender, and turn toward Him (repentance), is God's terms for the transformation of your inner self-life, according to the best selling book in the world, His Word:

That if you confess with your mouth [that's admission] **the Lord Jesus** [that title, **Lord**, means a surrender and a turn to His authority, His Lordship], **and believe in your heart that God has raised Him from the dead, you will be saved. For with the heart one believes unto righteousness, and with the mouth confession is made unto salvation...For whoever calls on the name of the Lord shall be saved.** –Romans 10:9-10, 13

It's amazing when you think it through: the One who is going to defeat you is the same One who is offering you a pardon from your sin judgment and a new position in His eternal Kingdom. Perhaps a simple written prayer can guide you in what your heart needs to say:

"Dear God, I want to be changed. I confess to You that I am a sinner, controlled by worldly characteristics. I realize that I have broken your law and that puts me under Your just condemnation. I don't want Your wrath—I want and need Your mercy and forgiveness. I surrender my all to You and I repent.

"I believe that You and Jesus are alive and will come to live in me by Your Holy Spirit. I ask You to forgive me and to come into me now and make me a new creation—**transform me!** Based on Your promises and on Your terms, I yield to Your Spirit's inner transformation that will form Your spiritual traits in my new nature. Thank You, God, for saving me, in Jesus' name, amen."

Admit, confess, repent, and surrender: these are the initial steps into inner spiritual transformation. Don't take this lightly and don't leave this transforming chapter until you fully understand what can occur or what has just occurred. Now the next chapter introduces you to the steps of testing your new spiritual "wings."

Additional Bible verses: (Note the character traits that refer to being **transformed**.)

> John 1:12 – **But as many as received Him, to them He gave the right to become children of God, to those who believe in His name.**

> 1 Corinthians 6:19-20 – **Or do you not know that your body is the temple of the Holy Spirit who is in you, whom**

you have from God, and you are not your own? For you were bought at a price; therefore glorify God in your body and in your spirit, which are God's.

2 Corinthians 5:14-15 – **For the love of Christ compels us, because we judge thus: that if One died for all, then all died; and He died for all, that those who live should live no longer for themselves, but for Him who died for them and rose again.**

Philippians 1:21-24 – **For to me, to live is Christ, and to die is gain. But if I live on in the flesh, this will mean fruit from my labor; yet what I shall choose I cannot tell. For I am hard-pressed between the two, having a desire to depart and be with Christ, which is far better. Nevertheless to remain in the flesh is more needful for you.**

Philippians 3:15-16 – **Therefore let us, as many as are mature, have this mind; and if in anything you think otherwise, God will reveal even this to you. Nevertheless, to the degree that we have already attained, let us walk by the same rule, let us be of the same mind.**

CHAPTER 10 ~ The End is Near

If you meant what you may have just prayed in the previous chapter, you can be assured that God and Jesus reside in you by the Holy Spirit. According to Jesus, you have, just now, passed from spiritual death into a new spiritual life. The transformation takes place when you admit, confess, repent, and surrender yourself to God through Jesus Christ. Read carefully what Jesus says:

Most assuredly, I say to you, he who hears My word [are you listening?] **and believes in Him who sent Me has everlasting life** [present tense]**, and shall not come into judgment** [present tense]**, but has passed from death into life** [perfect tense: a Greek verb tense that means, completed in the past with continued results]. –John 5:24

Paraphrased, the above verse may read:

"You can count on what I say to you: he who **hears** My word and understands what I'm saying, and commits himself to God who sent Me, is transformed **into a state of everlasting life**, and beginning right now, **shall never** come into judgment, because he **has been transformed from death into a continual state of eternal life.**"

This is the end...the beginning end! You've "died" to your old self-life—you've ended the self-centered life—and can now move on in your newfound life in Jesus Christ. You are now living on a new level with Christ. You now have the Holy Spirit of the living

God dwelling in you to assist you along the way of your new life. You can now return to the preceding chapters and apply all the inner character traits discussed with the help of the Holy Spirit of God and Jesus residing in you. The character traits discussed previously are just a portion of all the benefits of a new life in Christ (cf. Galatians 5:22-23; Ephesians 6:10-20).

The Holy Spirit will begin to remold your inner self into the likeness of Christ. There is a lot to read and learn from God's Word. His Word will be the resource that the Spirit will use as you begin to have **the mind of Christ** (1 Corinthians 2:16). Remember, a genuine surrender to God, through Jesus, means you become an obedient servant to His Word and His will. As you yield to Him, He begins to lead you into a wonderful life that will characterize His nature.

What's next? First of all, I recommend you review each previous chapter and begin a slow but deliberate effort to yield to God's Spirit as he applies each trait explained. From each chapter, write out some immediate tangible steps to take that reveal your new nature. Here's an example:

Chapter 1 – Joyful

This is what I can do to become a more joyful person:
1. Stop criticizing my children.
2. Look at the positive points in my co-workers.
3. Go for a walk with my spouse.
4. Study the extra Bible verses at the end of the chapter.
5. Load my brains before I shoot my mouth.
6. (Add your own.)

Do this with each chapter. Put each list on a 3 x 5 card to keep with you at all times. Ask God's Spirit to help you. Place each card in a strategic place throughout your home, school, automobile, or workplace as a constant reminder. You should jot down the Bible verses from each chapter on cards also. Keep them handy; memorize them.

Also, you should immediately seek out other genuine believers in a Bible-teaching and Bible-preaching church. Bible study and

ಬ THE END IS NEAR ೞ

Bible-centered preaching are very important to spiritual growth. So make sure the Bible is the main resource book used for all teaching and preaching. As a new follower of Jesus, you will want to get baptized because your Lord commands this of you (cf. Matt. 28:18-20).

As a transformed follower, you should go to church every week to receive further instruction from God's Word (cf. Hebrews 10:25). Go with the determination to be an infectious Christian. That means you are going to infect others with genuine Christianity by helping them experience the satisfaction of being **Transformed!**

Oh, and don't forget to tell your face to express **the new you!!**

Additional Bible verses: (Note the character traits that refer to a **secure, eternal life**.)

John 10:28-29 – **And I give them eternal life, and they shall never perish; neither shall anyone snatch them out of My hand. My Father, who has given them to Me, is greater than all; and no one is able to snatch them out of My Father's hand.**

1 John 5:12-13 – **He who has the Son has life; he who does not have the Son of God does not have life. These things I have written to you who believe in the name of the Son of God, that you may know that you have eternal life, and that you may continue to believe in the name of the Son of God.**

Transformed!

Transformed!

~

Part Two

~

The Marriage

Dedication

To my mom, Mildred Ruth Burke Jones Stokes, who I love very much and is very special to me;

To my wife, Diane, who has given me unspeakable joy and happiness;

To my children and their families who are making the silver years so enjoyable; and,

To all followers of Jesus Christ who hunger for that intimate spiritual relationship displayed throughout the Scriptures,

I dedicate this section.

PART TWO

Transformed! – Let the Relationship Begin!

The journey into inner change continues with a deeper look into the nature of a maturing, inner, spiritual transformation. The next section of this book allows you to continue the transformation by discovering the intimacy involved with God as a follower of Jesus. **PART TWO** will reveal to you that genuine Christianity is the formation of a personal relationship with God and Jesus Christ. Only through an intimate relationship can you understand what a complete transformation from within is all about. Note the following comparison of the two:

If <u>*PART ONE*</u>	Then <u>*PART TWO*</u>
Is conception…	…Is life
Is the wedding day…	…Is the marriage
Is the "old" nature…	…Is the "new" nature
Is the O.T. covenants…	…Is the N.T. covenant
Is the 2 fish and 5 loaves…	…Is the feeding of the 5,000
Is the "milk" of the Word…	…Is the "meat" of the Word

You need PART TWO of this book—for what is the evidence of conception except life? Or what is a wedding without a marriage? There is more to a spiritual life than just to be "born again." As our physical life was designed for an intimate relationship, so our spiritual life was designed for an intimate relationship with our Creator God through Jesus Christ our Lord. Don't stay at the spiritual altar; go on to enjoy the "honeymoon" and new relationship you now have with your Savior and God. Read the following pages and discover the joy and power of God's presence.

Part Two ~ The Marriage

Contents

Foreword	*by Ed Ethridge*	61
Introduction	*Transformed for Intimacy!*	63
Chapter 1	*God Speaks to Me*	71
Chapter 2	*In God's Presence*	79
Chapter 3	*Baptism – A Symbol of Intimacy*	87
Chapter 4	*The Gift That Keeps Giving*	95
Chapter 5	*Now Faith Is...*	101
Chapter 6	*Am I Worth a Million Bucks or What?!*	107
Chapter 7	*Forty Days That Changed the World*	111
Chapter 8	*Why is God in Me?*	119
Chapter 9	*The Priesthood of Man*	125
Chapter 10	*A Dark River Flows Nearby*	131
Chapter 11	*Possessed*	135
Chapter 12	*But, What If...?*	143
Chapter 13	*Fellowship*	147
Chapter 14	*Abide in Me*	151
Chapter 15	*Mission Possible*	155
Chapter 16	*Circumcision – 'A Sign of the Covenant'*	161
Postscript		167

Transformed!

FOREWORD ~ PART TWO

Intimacy with God among believers is trying to keep pace with the loss of intimacy among married couples. Why is the divorce rate as great inside the church as outside the church? Could this be due to the lack of understanding of a believer's intimacy with God?

Second Corinthians 5:17 says, **If any man be in Christ, he is a new creation...** The idea of a new creation is foreign to the average Christian. They fail to correlate their new location, as a new creation, as being in Christ. And because of that, they fail to comprehend the mandates of Christ our Lord to live godly, holy, pure, joyful, and obedient lives. Therefore, the majority plod along, knee deep in the shallow and stagnant cesspools of immaturity, thinking that Christian maturity is a reformation of a dead religion.

In reality, there is no reality! Why is the average confessing believer floundering in the quagmire of futility, frustration, and faithlessness? I am fully persuaded it is due to shallow teaching. There's shallowness in the pulpit and shallowness in the classroom. Story-telling preaching that fails to scratch the surface of a biblical text produces an infantile mindset and the reality seen is that of Revelation 3:1: **...I know your works, that you have a name that you are alive, but you are dead.**

In *Transformed!* ~ **PART TWO**, Johnnie Jones has made a direct hit on the issue of immaturity in Christians and in the church. As a pastor for thirty-three years and my personal friend since 1974,

ಬು Transformed! ಆ

Johnnie has been a stalwart of influence and encouragement in my life and in the lives of many believers. He is convinced that genuine Christianity is evidenced in the format of an intimate relationship with a holy God through Jesus Christ. I commend you to this same discovery as you read the following pages. My prayer is that there will be a desire within you for a continual transformation and may it be all for His great Glory.

Ed J. Ethridge, Director of Missions
North Texas Baptist Area
Lewisville, Texas

[Previously written in **Metamorphosis 2: The Transforming Power of Intimacy With God;** © 2004. *Some statements are updated to conform to the year 2010.]*

INTRODUCTION ~ PART TWO

Transformed for Intimacy

> **So God created man in His own image, in the image of God He created him; male and female He created them....**
> **But for Adam there was not found a helper comparable to him....**
> **Then the rib which the LORD God had taken from man He made into a woman, and He brought her to the man.**
> –Genesis 1:27; 2:20c, 22

You have read **PART ONE**. Now you should be anxious to read more about this new spiritual transformation. It's time to commune in the love of God and in the grace of Jesus Christ, whom you call your Lord (2 Corinthians 13:14). A very important step is needed at this point: **do not mimic the Christians around you!** Jesus is **your** Lord and He wants **you** to follow Him in developing this new relationship. You'll understand this important step as you read further; but for now, allow me to make a serious statement:

Many Christians have lost intimacy with their God and Savior. They have done so through an exchange of a relationship for a religion.

God is a God of relationships. He created all living things in such a way that they would relate with each other. He created you and me as relational beings. Created in the image of God, we have many levels of relationships—some physical and some spiritual. We survive on the earth through physical relationships. There are friends, siblings, co-workers, spouses, etc. We live and have purpose through relationships.

Followers of Jesus Christ are told that they have a spiritual relationship with God, through Jesus, by the power of His Holy Spirit. The Holy Spirit is said to indwell the life of every follower. There are many reasons why God set up the indwelling presence of His Spirit. His presence gives followers peace, joy, assurance of heaven, and a host of other feelings and promises. But I believe the primary reason for the indwelling presence is to develop an intimate relationship with God—a relationship beyond the surface benefits of being a Christian. It is this level of relationship through which we find our purpose as Christians. However, spiritual intimacy with God requires a number of prerequisites before such an encounter can be achieved. God is holy and pure and, therefore, cannot co-mingle with man unless change occurs from within that man. The initial change is described in the Scriptures as being born again: **Unless one is born again, he cannot enter the kingdom of God** (Jesus in John 3:3). This is discussed in **PART ONE** of this book.

The ongoing transformation in a spiritual relationship with God is called a metamorphosis:

> **I beseech you therefore, brethren, by the mercies of God, that you present your bodies a living sacrifice, holy, acceptable to God, which is your reasonable service. And do not be conformed to this world, but be transformed** [metamorphosed] **by the renewing of your mind, that you may prove what is that good and acceptable and perfect will of God.** –Romans 12:1-2

The word, **transformed**, is *metamorphoō** in its original Greek form and is descriptive of the change that must occur from within. That's where intimacy occurs and that's what spiritual transformation is all about. According to Romans 12:1-2 (above),

ಐ Introduction ~ Part Two ಚ

this transformation is part of a spiritual process that every follower of Jesus Christ is to initiate in order to experience a deeper relationship with God. **Conformed to this world** literally means to fashion or pattern your character to a world standard, a standard that contradicts a godly nature.

God commands every follower of Jesus Christ to be transformed. There is no option; it is the natural response a follower will have as his desire for a relationship with God matures. But spiritual transformation requires a follower to respond to God in the context of a limited physical body. However, when one begins to allow an inner transformation, God's Spirit begins to pursue spiritual depth in a Christian's life, thus fulfilling the command of Romans 12:1-2.

In **Part One** of *Transformed!* I introduce the initial change process of a genuine spiritual transformation that can occur in a person, based on the New Testament. This initial process is the act of God uncovering, reviving, and transforming basic character traits found in fallen mankind. The revived character traits are described as the **fruit of the Spirit** in Galatians 5:22-23. These traits not only allow the formation of a civilized environment, but also allow the eternal nature of God to commune with man.

Spiritual transformation occurs in the inner spirit (or soul) of a man and is the mechanism by which God enters a person and matures him. The initial act of God's Spirit is to enter into the soul of a person that has surrendered his self-control over to God. This placement allows the Holy Spirit to transform and control an individual by giving birth to a new spirit in that person's soul. This new spiritual birth is the event that separates Christianity from all other religions. In fact, as you read on, you will discover that this new spiritual birth divides the "religion" of Christianity from the living of Christianity. This relational drive of God will become more apparent as you read further in this volume.

I purposely wrote **Part One** as a concise introduction of the initial stage to an awakened inner spiritual nature. I use part of the **fruit of the Spirit** (cf. Gal. 5:22-23) as the basic benefits of a transformed nature. That's why the beginning chapters are very positive and encouraging in the descriptions of basic character traits. The "how to" in the change process is written near the end of **PART ONE**. But its end is really just the beginning of a new birth. More must be written to help a follower understand how spiritual formation and maturity develops during this process. This new birth must be nurtured and that's where **PART TWO** fits into the process.

PART TWO

In this section, I introduce the maturing experiences of a transforming spiritual nature that was conceived at the moment of salvation—that moment when a person voluntarily commits his life to a relationship with Jesus Christ. Life begins at conception; thus a new spiritual life begins at the conception of genuine salvation. But, as in a physical conception, there is still a period of inner development, a period of gestation. It is during this spiritual gestation period that an individual begins to form into the nature from which he was conceived. This spiritual gestation period takes on a unique personal process within that, in time, results in a transformed Godly nature.

Many Christians misunderstand the process—the transformation—of the new birth. Many treat their salvation experience—their conception into Christianity—as the whole birth process. But, in fact, it takes a period of time for a follower of Christ to develop spiritual transformation that leads to an intimate, ongoing relationship with Christ. It does not have to take a long time, but each follower's developmental stage—gestation period— is based on a number of conditions. For example, some followers may attend a language school or other preparatory educational facility in order to fulfill their ministry. Others will develop, over time, as they attend church or participate in personal or group Bible study. Some may simply choose to remain immature. God allows choice, even though He commands all followers to mature—to gestate—in the disciplines of Christianity. For example:

That we should no longer be children, tossed to and fro and carried about with every wind of doctrine, by the trickery of men, in the cunning craftiness of deceitful plotting, but, speaking the truth in love, *may grow up in all things into*

ೂ Introduction ~ Part Two ಚ

Him **who is the head—Christ—** (Ephesians 4:14-15; emphasis added). **But *grow* in the grace and knowledge of our Lord and Savior Jesus Christ.** –2 Peter 3:18 (emphasis added)

When Jesus walked about during His ministry on earth, He often revealed the process of spiritual transformation within His sayings and by His actions. For example, when people asked Jesus when the kingdom of God would come, He replied, **the kingdom of God is within you** (Luke 17:21). People were looking for a physical change, but Jesus was pointing to an inner transformation for mankind. He explained that, although this physical earth would have to undergo its own physical transformation, the revelation of His spiritual kingdom would start with a spiritual transformation from within each follower and eventually consummate in a transformation of the physical world.

Jesus once said,

Do not labor for the food which perishes, but for the food which endures to everlasting life, which the Son of Man will give you, because God the Father has set His *seal* on Him (John 6:27, emphasis added).

The **seal** was the spiritual life inside Jesus given to Him by the Father (John 5:26). As **Son of Man**, Jesus lived an exemplary life for His followers as He revealed the spiritual world around them and His relationship with His Father. He lived in total dependence of His Father in whom was His life. He downplayed the physical manifestations of God's power in Him because He did not come to earth in the flesh to set up a physical replica of God's presence; He came **to seek and to save that which was lost** (Luke 19:10). He said, **I have not come to call the righteous, but sinners to repentance** (Luke 5:32). He was after their hearts. After discovering and converting a handful of disciples, Jesus began to develop them through a revelation of the spiritual world. This revelation and its intimate expression in the life of a follower of Jesus is the apex of this book.

In **Part Two**, a follower will be challenged and taught how to experience a deeper level of oneness with the Triune God within himself. This oneness will be revealed as the key to an inner life of spiritual power. As a follower experiences the oneness of the Trinity, he will also understand why much of modern Christianity is spiritually inept due to an emphasis, by some, on physical accomplishments or organized religion as evidences of Christian maturity. For many, accomplishments, such as church attendance, become the fulfillment of the purpose of one's spiritual life. Yet physical accomplishments were a lessened emphasis with Jesus. In fact, He was so wearied with everyone asking for physical signs and miracles that He said, perhaps often, that **a wicked and adulterous generation seeks after a sign...** (Matthew 16:4), and, **unless you people see signs and wonders, you will by no means believe** (John 4:48; cf. Matthew 12:39; Mark 8:12; Luke 11:29; 1 Corinthians 1:22-29). Instead of walking around and firing off miracles at random, Jesus devoted most of His ministry on earth teaching and training His followers how to live and develop an intimate spiritual life within themselves in spite of the physical accomplishments that may or may not occur. He tried to steer His disciples away from measuring spiritual accomplishments with physical results. That's because the physical is just that—physical.

PART TWO is written to help you discover the true purpose and depth of your spiritual life on earth. You will be introduced to the command for you to "die daily" in Jesus Christ (cf. 1 Corinthians 15:31; Colossians 3:3). This is the "presentation" part of Romans 12:1-2. Then you will be challenged to transform your life in such a way that will mirror the exemplary life of Jesus. If you are willing to transform your mind, as a follower of Jesus, you will **prove what is that good and acceptable and perfect will of God** (Rms. 12: 2); and you will live out all that is written of a follower of Jesus in the Scriptures.

Can this level of spiritual intimacy be experienced while here on earth? Can the physical body yield itself to the transforming power of the spiritual level of understanding that I describe? Can the Spirit of God enter a person and truly dominate and alter his or her existence? These are some of the questions I will attempt to answer because there is more to the living of Christianity than many followers are experiencing. Every follower of Jesus will be

ೞ Introduction ~ Part Two ೫

challenged to rethink his or her communication and communion with God in the real spiritual world. So don't look around you for a relational pattern...look into Jesus and into His Word. Study His relationship with the Father for your relational pattern.

PART TWO will lead you into a more in-depth understanding of a follower's lifestyle with a holy God. It will reveal many of the spiritual qualities a transformed person experiences and expresses in union with Holy God and Jesus Christ. It will also describe the Spirit's ability to enter a follower's spirit to alter the soul. That's where the transformation occurs. As you read, you will begin to distinguish the difference between a natural soul-relationship with Jesus from a spiritual soul-relationship. I will explain the difference between the two and how a natural soul-relationship is not the ultimate purpose of **Christ in you** [as] **the hope of glory** (Colossians 1:27). Understanding the differences between the natural and spiritual control of the soul is necessary to discover the purpose and beauty of your life in union with God in the spiritual world.

As you may have noticed, I usually describe a Christian as a "follower" of Jesus. I prefer this term rather than "believer," to emphasize action rather than mental acceptance. Obviously, followers of Jesus are believers; but many "believe" in Jesus and **even the demons believe—and tremble!** (James 2:19) A mental awareness or acknowledgement of Jesus has never saved a soul. There must be an act involved—an intimate act—for conception to occur. And, there must be continued intimacy and interaction with the Holy Spirit of God in order for your relationship to mature in the spiritual world.

Also, I am writing **PART TWO** to you as to a follower—as one who has experienced genuine spiritual birth. In other words, spiritual conception has occurred. Therefore, as a follower of Jesus, the most important tool you must rely upon inside the spiritual world is the Holy Spirit within you. He is your only spiritual connection from within. Listen to Him. Learn to trust His guidance as you go deeper within yourself to transform the soul's nature in which you were born. The Holy Spirit is the only living spiritual agent who can renew your mind to interpret and apply God's Word in your new world. He's the only One who can take you beyond the intuition of your natural soul into the innermost part of your being where the Spirit of God dwells, thus allowing spiritual communication, revelation, understanding, and strength.

Communication is the key to developing an intimate relationship. So how you communicate with the Holy Spirit will be explained first. Do not rush through this most important step of how God's Spirit communicates within you. He is your only lifeline to the truth. God has an intense desire to reveal the truth of the nature of both the physical world and the spiritual world in which you now live. If, after reading the first chapter you do not perceive the communication of God's Holy Spirit within you, I advise you to proceed with caution as you continue reading. I do not want to frustrate you or cause you to try and counterfeit the spiritual attributes of God within your soul's senses. That's why the first chapter teaches you how to communicate with God. This is the key that unlocks all the doors of spiritual maturity. Comprehend and master its instructions to your Spirit-controlled nature.

---

* (Page 64) Greek words are transliterated from Strong's Concordance, A Dictionary of the Greek Testament, James Strong, Hendrickson Publishers, Peabody, MA; n.d.

CHAPTER 1 ~ God Speaks to Me

Then God said... –Genesis 1:3

Call to Me, and I will answer you, and show you great and mighty things, which you do not know. –Jeremiah 33:3

God speaks over a thousand times to Israel in the Old Testament. He persistently presents Himself as the God who wants to communicate with His people. He was constantly trying to lead them to be a cut above the rest of the world. Even today, God wants to talk to His followers and to show them some **great and mighty things**. He wants to tell them things they don't know.

If you are a follower of Jesus Christ, think for a moment Who it is that wants to talk to you. Listen again to the Almighty God as you read Jeremiah 33:3 in this paraphrase: *"Speak to me and I will speak to you; and when I speak, I will reveal powerful things in and through your life that will be amazing and difficult to comprehend."*

Jesus also says something similar:
Until now you have asked nothing in My name. Ask, and you will receive, that your joy may be full. –John 16:24

Just as communication is essential for social or personal growth and development, spiritual communication is essential for spiritual growth and development. The only difference is that the spiritual message is spoken through an inner consciousness of God's Spirit within you, explaining His Word to you. The Spirit of God energizes the written Word of God to speak to you. Look at the following two verses and **note what the Spirit can say to you when you listen:**

> **However, when He, the Spirit of truth, has come, He will guide you into all truth...whatever He hears He will speak; and He will tell you things to come...All things that the Father has are Mine. Therefore I said that He will take of Mine and declare** [speak] **it to you.** –Jesus, in John 16:13, 15

Truth—that's what the Spirit speaks and that's what everyone needs to hear from Him. You don't need a volume of false promises or a room full of relative thoughts. You need to hear and know the truth of God. When God speaks, He speaks truth. Jesus said He came only to do what God told Him to do and nothing else (John 5:30; 8:38). Jesus spoke God's truth and He wants you to receive, understand, and speak God's truth.

The problem is, most people—and many Christians—won't take the time to have God reveal His truth to them. Communication involves a two-way conversation. The most important question this author can ask you is: **Are you hearing from God when you speak to Him?**

People can be so impatient, can't they? Also, many have bought into the relativity of truth in such a way that it is near impossible for them to hear God's truth. His truth can be heard and understood, but there are a few conditions established by God in order to hear from Him. For example, note in the following verses the word or words that describe what people need to do to hear from God:

> **Be still and know that I am God.** –Psalm 46:10a

> **But those who wait on the Lord shall renew their strength.**
> –Isaiah 40:31a

～ God Speaks to Me ～

Behold, I stand at the door and knock. If anyone hears My voice and opens the door, I will come in to him and dine with him, and he with Me...He who has an ear, let him hear what the Spirit says to the churches. –Revelation 3:20, 22

If I regard iniquity in my heart, the Lord will not hear. –Psalm 66:18

What do the above verses tell you that you need to do to hear from God? You should at least recognize that you must be still and wait on God. Plus, He wants to stay with you long enough for "dining" to occur. You must also deal with **iniquity** in your life. Then, when He speaks, you should open the door of that place within you where you perceive God's Spirit residing and let Him and His word occupy your inner being. This inner fellowship (**dine**, in Revelation 3:20) is essential for God to speak to you. This is when, where, and how you can hear God speak deep truths to you.

At this point, a couple more questions ought to be answered by you: (1) Have you transformed the patience of your soul that is necessary to allow your spirit to wait and listen to His Spirit? And, (2) Do you even want to hear from God?

These are two important questions to ponder within yourself because the human side of you will resist this command to be still and listen for God to speak to your inner being. The act of surrendering your soul into an inner submissive role to the Spirit of God is difficult, near impossible, from a human standpoint. Yet the Scriptures are replete with this specific basic command to be still and listen to God. To nail down the importance of this command, I recommend you look at the following verses in your Bible that refer to speaking, listening, or hearing, as it pertains to your communication with God. These are just a sampling of many such verses: Matthew 10:19-20, 32-33; 17:1-5; Mark 4:21-25; Isaiah 49:1-6; 65:12; Psalm 50:7-15; 85:8; John 15:26-27; 16:12-15.

When you read the above verses, they will help you discover that God still speaks today and He's waiting for you to slow down

enough to listen to Him. Nothing else in the process of spiritual transformation is as important as this understanding and activity. This is how an intimate relationship begins. Nothing else makes Christianity so understandable and so enjoyable on this earth as having the Creator God speak to His followers by His indwelling Spirit through His Word. **The greatest spiritual asset you have, as a follower of Jesus, is having God live inside you. It is within this access that you can speak with God and God speaks to you.**
Understanding your access into the presence of God will help you understand the ability to speak to God. Let's read a little more about this access.

Access To Holy God

For through Him [Jesus] **we both have access by one Spirit to the Father.** –Ephesians 2:18

You cannot develop a maturing relationship with anyone unless that person grants you access into his or her personal world. This is exactly what God has done for you; you now have personal access to God. The above verse says that this access is **through Him**. The **Him** is referring to Jesus Christ. Now I want you to look carefully at the context of this verse. As you read Ephesians 2:14-18, note the how and the why God has granted you access:

For He Himself is our peace, who has made both one [i.e., **the commonwealth of Israel and strangers from the covenants of promise** (v. 12)], **and has broken down the middle wall of separation, having abolished in His flesh the enmity, that is, the law of commandments contained in ordinances, so as to create in Himself one new man from the two, thus making peace, and that He might reconcile them both to God in one body through the cross, thereby putting to death the enmity. And He came and preached peace to you who were afar off and to those who were near. For through Him we both have access by one Spirit to the Father.** –Ephesians 2:14-18 (cf. v. 19-22)

Did you note the repetitive word, **peace**? This is the resultant benefit of a follower's encounter with His God. In fact, the

Ephesians context is speaking directly to the peace Jewish and non-Jewish followers will experience among themselves. This was foretold in God's Word:

> **Nevertheless the gloom will not be upon her who is distressed, as when at first He lightly esteemed the land of Zebulun and the land of Naphtali, and afterward more heavily oppressed her, by the way of the sea, beyond the Jordan, in Galilee of the Gentiles. The people who walked in darkness have seen a great light; those who dwelt in the land of the shadow of death, upon them a light has shined.**
> –Isaiah 9:1-2

> **But it is not that the word of God has taken no effect. For they are not all Israel who are of Israel, nor are they all children because they are the seed of Abraham; but, "In Isaac your seed shall be called." That is, those who are the children of the flesh, these are not the children of God; but the children of the promise are counted as the seed.**
> –Romans 9:6-8

> **For you are all sons of God through faith in Christ Jesus. For as many of you as were baptized into Christ have put on Christ. There is neither Jew nor Greek, there is neither slave nor free, there is neither male nor female; for you are all one in Christ Jesus. And if you are Christ's, then you are Abraham's seed, and heirs according to the promise.**
> –Galatians 3:26-29

These verses, and many more, reveal that there is only one way to have access with the Father—it is through Jesus Christ. The former separate approach to God, whether Jew or non-Jew, has now been put into one way. Access to God is not dependent on a religion or a nationality. It is dependent upon a person—the person of Jesus Christ. Jesus has given you an audience with God the Father.

But why have access to God? What would be your reason or need for access to God? And why does God even bother to provide you an access to Him? Two additional passages will help you:

> **For as many as are led by the Spirit of God, these are the sons of God. For you did not receive the spirit of bondage again to fear, but you received the Spirit of adoption by whom we cry out, "Abba, Father." The Spirit Himself bears witness with our spirit that we are children of God, and if children, then heirs—heirs of God and joint heirs with Christ, if indeed we suffer with Him, that we may also be glorified together.** –Romans 8:14-17

And: **But when the fullness of the time had come, God sent forth His Son, born of a woman, born under the law, to redeem those who were under the law, that we might receive the adoption as sons. And because you are sons, God has sent forth the Spirit of His Son into your hearts, crying out, "Abba, Father!" Therefore you are no longer a slave but a son, and if a son, then an heir of God through Christ.**
–Galatians 4:4-7

From these passages you see a follower calling God, **Abba, Father**. Most Bible scholars agree that this phrase is a term of endearment. This means that God relates to the followers of Jesus Christ as a dear Father. As an endearing Father, God wants to talk to His children when they're in His presence. He seeks an intimate relationship with you; and it begins by communicating with Him.

Standing Before God

Let's look at Romans 5:1-2 to discover the concept of having a communicative relationship with God:

> **Therefore, having been justified by faith, we have peace with God through our Lord Jesus Christ, through whom we also have access by faith into this grace in which we stand, and rejoice in the hope of the glory of God.**

ঙ God Speaks to Me ೧ಽ

This passage is pregnant with descriptive words of having an intimate relationship with God. First of all, being **justified by faith** denotes your submissive step into the relationship based on what God has declared. God has declared followers of Jesus as **justified**, and they enter into this declaration of justification **by faith**. **By faith** is your act of moving into an intimate relationship with the Father. **Grace** describes God's willingness to receive you in such a relationship. It is a merciful and loving act of God toward anyone who turns to Him through Jesus. **Peace** is the effect of a **justified** follower standing in God's presence through His **grace**. The result is rejoicing **in the hope** [confidence] **of the glory** [presence] **of God**. So God, through Jesus Christ, has invited you into a special position with Him in order for intimate communication to occur.

This passage, along with Ephesians 2:18 (above), gives good indication that God wants to relate to you, as a follower of His Son. In fact, the very word **Father** is indicative of how He wants you to perceive His relationship with Him as you stand before Him. Ideally speaking, His fatherhood tells you that He will provide for you, protect you, and love you. His love is described as being **poured out in our hearts by the Holy Spirit who was given to us** (Romans 5:5). This is the **glory** of His fatherhood: His **Holy Spirit who was given to us**, manifests Him in you.

So how should you respond in His presence? God wants you to respond with confidence in Him—enough confidence to speak to Him regularly. He wants you to respond to Him as a loving Father and to talk freely and openly with Him. This is your greatest asset as a follower: **having a God who loves you and wants to speak to you**, especially when there is a need. You do have needs, don't you? Children have constant needs. You, as a follower of Jesus, are a child of God and have constant spiritual needs. And your Heavenly Father has a plan for meeting your needs. Let's devote another chapter to understanding this. But before you go any further, answer these two questions:

✞ **Do you understand that God speaks to you?**

✞ **Do you understand how He does this and how you must prepare for intimate communication to occur?**

Listen to Him speak to you again: **Be still and know that I am God** (Psalm 46:10a). Use the access you have to God through His Holy Spirit. **Speak to Him**. Begin to have conversations with God every day. This is called, prayer. Believe His statements that He wants you to talk to Him…then let His Word talk back to you. Don't just read the Bible; let His Holy Spirit take His written Word and provide spiritual nourishment for your soul. **Let Him speak to you!**

It is essential that you have a daily interaction of prayer with God. You must devote time to speak to your Father and allow time for Him to speak to you. If you cannot do this, then you may as well close this book, put it on a shelf, and try to live a religion of Christianity—not a genuine intimate relationship with God, as He intended. There is a big difference and as you continue to read you will discover this essential difference.

CHAPTER 2 ~ In God's Presence

A follower of Jesus Christ is still a sinner. As long as you have air and blood flowing in you and as long as there is a devil, you will be subject to temptations in the flesh. So how can a follower maintain a continual position in the presence of God? It is found in the new position of Christ before the Father. He is described as a follower's High Priest:

> **Seeing then that we have a great High Priest who has passed through the heavens, Jesus the Son of God, let us hold fast our confession. For we do not have a High Priest who cannot sympathize with our weaknesses, but was in all points tempted as we are, yet without sin. Let us therefore come boldly to the throne of grace, that we may obtain mercy and find grace to help in time of need.** –Hebrews 4:14-16

Simply stated, Jesus' position and action, as High Priest, has provided the access you have before God. As High Priest, Jesus eliminates any obstacle between you and your Father. Without Jesus, God would be as unapproachable as He was under the Old Covenant; but through Jesus, God sits on a **throne of grace**. Therefore in this passage you, as a follower of Jesus, are told to **come boldly** into God's presence.

A look at Hebrews 10:19-23 explains this bold approach further. This passage explains the endearment involved in this bold access. It says, in part, **...having boldness to enter the Holiest by the blood of Jesus...let us draw near.** God has provided you a unique relationship with Him through Jesus Christ. You have access to His holy presence through the sacrifice of His uniquely born Son who became your High Priest. Jesus was not only the High Priest to present the sacrifice to God in your behalf, but strange as it may sound, He also became the sacrifice presented.

God's love allowed the sacrifice of His dear Son so that you could have a relationship with Him and speak to Him. His love is deeper than you or I can fathom; it is, nevertheless, God's way of saying, "Come to me; I want to talk with you." He wants to talk with you, and His Spirit speaks to you in and through His Word. So open the pages of God's Word and listen to Him speak. **So then faith comes by hearing, and hearing by the word of God.** –Romans 10:17

Come A Little Closer

When God speaks to you as a follower of His Son, it is not primarily to distinguish how great He is and how insignificant you are. He is not a Father who wants to bark orders at you. But to you, as His child, God speaks in such a manner as to draw you closer to Him. In Ephesians 2:11-13, you discover that, before you become a follower of Jesus Christ, you are described as outside of God's commonwealth. **But now in Christ Jesus you who once were far off have been brought near by the blood of Christ** (v. 13). The word, **near**, is the Greek word, *engoos*, which means, "within reach, so as to touch." It is derived from another Greek word, *agcho*, which means, "to squeeze." It carries the idea of coming together, of being embraced. God's presence is more than a casual appearance. His relationship with you is for the purpose of embracing you and becoming one with you.

The reason for this oneness is explained in the very next verses of Ephesians 2. Read verses 14-22 first, as a unit. Now notice several primary reasons for this oneness:

> ...**so as to create in Himself one new man from the two, thus making peace** (v. 15); ...**thereby putting to death the enmity** (v. 16); **For through Him** [Jesus] **we both have access by one Spirit to the Father** (v. 18); **Now, therefore, you are...fellow citizens with the saints and members of the household of God...in whom you also are being built together for a dwelling place of God in the Spirit** (v. 19, 22).

The **two**, once again, is referring to Jews and non-Jews becoming one with each other in Christ. With the fleshly barrier (ethnicity) removed, they are now **fellow citizens** and **are being built together for a dwelling place of God in the Spirit.** This oneness produces peace among His people and this oneness makes all followers of Christ equal members of His household with equal access to God. God makes use of this oneness in Christians—whether Jew or non-Jew—to form a **dwelling place** for Him in the Spirit. This **temple** (v. 21) is the place where God meets with man, accepts his sacrifice (which is himself (Rom.12:1-2)), destroys his separation from Him, and establishes a peaceful relationship. God established this oneness (nearness) with Him through the sacrificial act of Jesus Christ. He wants every follower of Christ to respond to His nearness that He may dwell with man.

Why don't we just naturally draw near to God? The answer lies with the sin in our flesh. Sin interferes with your oneness with God. The nature of your flesh pulls you out of your nearness with Him. This is normal because this is the nature of flesh—the natural man. But God is as close as your call to Him and has provided some steps for your return. Your return is a process that you must develop over time so that you won't stray too far away. God wants you to stay close to Him and stay longer with Him as you mature in your relationship. The way to develop and maintain your closeness with God is explained in the next verses.

ꙮ Transformed! ꙮ

Take a Bath

> **If we confess our sins, He is faithful and just to forgive us our sins and to cleanse us from all unrighteousness.** –1 John 1:9

> **Draw near to God and He will draw near to you. Cleanse your hands, you sinners; and purify your hearts, you double-minded.** –James 4:8

The above verses give you the key to maintaining your oneness—your intimacy—with God. Spiritual transformation is a process of intimacy; but there can be no oneness—no intimacy—with God (or fellow followers) unless you come to Him, first and foremost, in purity with sins forgiven. When sin is forgiven, your heart and your motives are purified and you can draw much closer to Him. God's holiness demands a clean and pure meeting for intimacy with Him. The Scriptures state that **as obedient children...as He who called you is holy, you also be holy in all your conduct, because it is written, "Be holy, for I am holy."** (1 Peter 1:14a, 15-16). In this context, **holy** means to be pure before God **in all your conduct**. The ongoing process of purity is called sanctification. To maintain purity requires you to have sin cleansed from your heart as often as necessary. Think of this process as you would of parents who prepare their children for a special family gathering. The parents will clean up the children, dress them in clean clothes, and remind them of their need to be on their best behavior. But children will be children, and a little dirt will show up. However, the parents don't interrupt the family gathering and leave just because a child made a mess (or two or three). The mess gets cleaned up as it occurs and the fellowship continues.

In God's Presence

The above passage from James (4:8) indicates that you must stop any physical or mental activity that may cause you to be defiled, thus separating you from God. You're also admonished to get your inner activity in step with Him (**purify your hearts**). Your mind must be in step with His. There can be no other gods before Him or anything that may cause a distraction. You cannot harbor sin in your heart and expect a meeting with God to occur without a conviction of that sin in your life and judgment upon it if you are unrepentant of it. It is His Spirit's duty to deal with sin at all times. That's why our High Priest (Jesus) is on duty at all times. First John 1:9 says, **If we confess our sins, He [Jesus] is faithful and just to forgive us our sins and to cleanse us from all unrighteousness.**

All the above is teaching a follower of Jesus that you can go before God at any time. He wants you to come near to Him, to be intimate with Him; but you must treat this intimacy—His nearness—as a holy encounter. So prepare for it and take a spiritual bath before the encounter.

Hold Fast the Confession

You are cleansed of sin by a repentant confession. In Hebrews 10:19-25, you will find several words for cleansing: **consecrated**, **sprinkled**, and **washed** (NKJV). These acts allow you to hold on to a **confession** of hope. God wants you to live in constant awareness that you are in His presence. You must hold fast to this confession; that is, you must believe it and behave it. When you perceive the presence of God in you, you will then act as in that presence. You will not act as you please; no, you will act as He pleases or you will act to please Him. Anything less is hypocrisy, unbelief, and disobedience. Anything less places you outside the perceived presence of God.

Stop Missing Church

Before you leave the above passage in Hebrews (Chapter 10), notice also the plurality of it. After several uses of the pronoun, **us**, this passage concludes:

☙ Transformed! ☙

And let us consider one another in order to stir up love and good works, not forsaking the assembling of ourselves together, as is the manner of some, but exhorting one another, and so much the more as you see the day approaching (10:24-25).

If called upon in the assembly of the church, each follower of Jesus should possess a word or an act of encouragement and/or exhortation. This is done **in order to stir up love and good works** (v. 24) among the followers. Now let's overlay this act and/or attitude with the command for followers to **draw near with a true heart in full assurance** (v. 22). The plurality is pointing to the necessity of togetherness in corporate worship with God. The whole phrase, **let us draw near**, is one Greek word, *proserchomai*, and means, "to come near to God" (as a group) in worship. It carries with it the idea of bowing down (prostrating) in honor of the presence of God.

In church, worship occurs when the corporate body is focused upon drawing near to God. It is His desire that His followers meet together as an act of worship. That's why this passage ends with a strong exhortation for followers to not forsake the **assembling of ourselves together, as is the manner of some...** (v. 25). Throughout the recorded history of God with man, one thing remains constant: **the command of God for His people to meet together in corporate worship**. This invites the nearness of God. Followers who avoid the **assembling** are disobeying a cardinal command of how God accepts worship. Remember, the dwelling place of God is within His temple and His temple is His people meeting together in corporate worship. In worship, you are confessing Him before others and you are experiencing the corporate presence of God as He is expressed within other followers.

Read the full passage of Hebrews 10:19-25 again. How important is it for followers to meet together in corporate worship? If you know this to be true and still ignore it, what does God say you are doing in the next verse: **For if we sin willfully after we have received the knowledge of the truth, there no longer remains a sacrifice for sins...** (v. 26). The full context is referring to the rejection of Jesus Christ, but you cannot dismiss the tie of this verse with the preceding exhortation to assemble with other followers. Do you sense the importance of corporate worship in this passage? Is it not because there is strength in numbers? And does it not help you, as an individual member—a building block—to see the rest of the "temple" experiencing the presence of the living God? It should.

All the worshiping, all the cleansing, and all the accesses into God's presence are for the express purpose of God wanting to speak to man—to you! God will speak to the one who will prepare for the encounter, the one who will seek personal cleansing and corporate worship. God doesn't take the encounter lightly and neither should you.

Evangelism

The corporate worship encounter also sheds light on the importance for you, as a member of God's fellowship of people, the church, to place a high priority on evangelism. Evangelism? That's right, evangelism. It is the initial act of calling all people (or any person), wherever you go, to be made right with God in order for a relationship to be established. In other words, everyone must take that initial spiritual bath before coming into God's presence. Through evangelism, you help initiate the first spiritual bath that every person must take to have a relationship with God. A positive response to this initial encounter with God is called salvation. After salvation occurs, subsequent cleansings occur during rededications and/or confessions of sin (1 John 1:9; cf., Ephesians 5:26). These confessions are ongoing acts for every follower and every local church in order to maintain a clean and pure relationship with God.

Speak to God? Take a bath? Have a relationship with Holy God? Corporate worship? Evangelism? Is all this necessary? If you want your relationship with God to deepen, the answer is YES! But you need to understand that there is a deeper motive from God for your personal encounter with Him. He did not sacrifice His only begotten Son in order to just establish visitation rights with you. We'll look further into this in the following chapters.

☙ Transformed! ☙

 Before you go any further, may I ask how you feel about this admonition to draw intimately closer to God? Remember, when you were first transformed (PART ONE), you became a **new creation** (2 Cor. 5:17). You are not approaching God alone, but through the blood of the sacrifice (Jesus) and by the power of the Holy Spirit. Don't be afraid, for you are not alone. The cleansing and the power to enter into God's presence are due to His existing Spirit dwelling within you. Now let's go a little further in the explanation of this spiritual transformation. In the next chapter, read slowly as you study a deep truth of your baptism.

CHAPTER 3 ~ Baptism – A Symbol of Intimacy

John's Gospel, the fourth book in the New Testament, contains a major prayer of Jesus in chapter seventeen. It is generally referred to as the high priestly prayer of Jesus because He is interceding in behalf of His followers. You should take time to read the whole chapter. However, for now, please read this excerpt:

I have manifested Your name to the men whom You have given Me out of the world. They were Yours, You gave them to Me, and they have kept Your word. Now they have known that all things which You have given Me are from You. For I have given to them the words which You have given Me; and they have received them, and have known surely that I came forth from You; and they have believed that You sent Me. I pray for them. I do not pray for the world but for those whom You have given Me, for they are Yours. And all Mine are Yours, and Yours are Mine, and I am glorified in them. Now I am no longer in the world, but these are in the world, and I come to You. Holy Father, keep through Your name those whom You have given Me, that they may be one as We are. While I was with them in the world, I kept them in Your name. Those whom You gave Me I have kept; and none of them is lost except the son of perdition, that the Scripture might be fulfilled. –John 17:6-12

☙ Transformed! ☙

As you read this carefully, you see a reoccurring word group: **given** and **gave**. (It may be helpful to underline them now.) Jesus is praying to the Father in behalf of the disciples whom God gave to Him. God gave the disciples to Jesus Christ for a continuation of His presence on the earth. In order for the disciples to continue this holy presence of God, they would need special positioning, training, and provisions. Jesus prays that they would recognize that God was the ultimate source of all things (v. 6, 7). Next, He prays they will recognize that His words are the same as God's words (v. 8). He then prays that they glorify God in their lives (v. 10). Jesus ends the prayer asking that God would keep His disciples as one in the world, just as He was one with the Father while He was in the world (v. 11). The keeping promise of this prayer would be a fulfillment of the Scriptures (v. 12).

Next, in John 17:20-26, Jesus shifts the prayer from the disciples to **those who will believe in Me through their** [the disciples'] **word** (v. 20). The Greek perfect tense verb* is used here, indicating an action completed in the past, but still carrying existing results. For example, the phrase, "It stands written." This portion of the prayer includes all followers of Jesus, beginning with the witness of the first disciples, to this present day.

Jesus prays primarily that His followers would remain as one in the keeping of His word, in manifesting His love, and in declaring the oneness of Jesus with the Father. He also prays that His followers will experience the glory invested in Him by His Father. This glory has always referred to the manifested presence of God before man. This oneness among the followers would prove to the world that Jesus and the Father were one (v. 22, 23). But how is it possible to maintain a clean and pure relationship with God, with Jesus, and with other followers of Jesus? How can your testimony about this oneness be maintained? The answer to these questions can be found in the word and act called **baptism**.

ɞ Baptism – A Symbol of Intimacy ʚ

The Baptism in Which to Reckon

The Greek word for baptism is *baptidzo* (from *bapto*). It literally means, "to make whelmed" (to infiltrate); that is, "to cover wholly" (like a garment that is dipped into a dye). The idea behind the word, baptize, is that which is baptized is now totally immersed into that which baptized. In other words, both the baptized and the element used in baptism are totally joined together and totally infiltrate each other, the element overwhelming the item immersed.

The element most people think of for baptism is water. Immersion into water is a good physical act to show the literal symbolism of baptism of an individual believer; however, water can only immerse a person externally. A physical baptism cannot fulfill the literal meaning of the word *baptidzo*, because water cannot fully whelm (infiltrate) the physical body. Water baptism, at its best, can only symbolize what occurs in spiritual baptism. Genuine spiritual baptism requires the total immersion of a person's inner being by— or, into—the Spirit of the living God. Spirit baptism goes into the spirit of a person, within his soul, and gives birth to a spiritual existence of God in that person.

How can this occur? Jesus performed a spiritual baptism upon His disciples right after He was resurrected: **"Peace to you! As the Father has sent Me, I also send you." And when He had said this, He breathed on them, and said to them, "Receive the Holy Spirit"** (John 20:21-22). When this breathing event occurred upon the disciples, it had immediate results, according to the Greek imperative verb tense used. It was a similar thing God did to the first man, Adam, **and breathed into his nostrils the breath of life; and man became a living being** (Genesis 2:7), right then and there. Spiritual baptism occurs when God breathes life back into a person. It is the total immersion (or infiltration) of God's **breath of life** into man. This baptism replaces the "death baptism" of sin in a person. Man was baptized into death through the first man's disobedience to God. This death is passed on to man through his physical nature at his physical conception: **Therefore, just as through one man sin entered the world,** and death through sin, and thus death spread to all men, because all sinned—... (Romans 5:12). Jesus came along and experienced this baptism of death in order to reverse the effect of man's baptism into death. Notice the explanation in the following verses:

> **How shall we who died to sin live any longer in it? Or do you not know that as many of us as were baptized into Christ Jesus were baptized into His death? Therefore we were buried with Him through baptism into death, that just as Christ was raised from the dead by the glory of the Father, even so we also should walk in newness of life.** –Romans 6:2b-4

Now notice the process that occurs: you are **baptized into His death**. This means you are totally immersed into the ramifications of Jesus' death. His death was for mankind's sin. His death was the requirement of God to satisfy the payment of sin (Romans 6:23). His death meant the surrender of His physical ability to save mankind. To be baptized into Jesus' death is to acknowledge a total surrender into His provision (sacrifice) for sin's atonement. You are releasing your life into His baptism of death. **For you died, and your life is hidden with Christ in God** (Colossians 3:3). **I have been crucified with Christ; it is no longer I who live, but Christ lives in me** (Galatians 2:20a).

Next you are **buried with Him through baptism into death**. This part of the baptism process indicates your helpless position as you allow yourself to be re-submerged into a covering of death (the water). You put yourself—your **old man** (nature; cf. Eph. 4:22-24; Col. 3:9-10)—into a spiritual grave. This acknowledges your complete dependency on another source for any future activity. A death and burial is a dramatic and conclusive ending of a previous nature of being. If you have doubts about this, ask any corpse in a coffin if things are different now.

At this point, baptism has done all it can do. You are completely immersed—you are buried into His death. The **old man** is crucified.

ೞ Baptism – A Symbol of Intimacy ೕ

If there is to be any more activity in your existence, there must be an intervention of power from another source. Can you raise yourself up out of a grave? No. Did Jesus? No. Well, Jesus once said that He had the power to lay down His life and the power to take it again (John 10:17-18); but even this statement was under the authority and power of His Father: **This command I have received from My Father** (10:18c). Additional Scriptures say that God the Father raised up Jesus from the dead (Romans 6:4; 10:9), indicating that the deliverance and resurrection of Jesus out of the grave and into a new life was under the authoritative command and power of God the Father.

Likewise, in your spiritual baptism, you are immersed in the death and burial of Jesus Christ, that just as He was raised from death by the glory of the Father, so you also must be raised by God's glory. This means that His presence and His power must invade your existence. You should symbolize this process by using water, as Jesus did (Matthew 3:16), but your spiritual baptism occurs when your inner spirit is resurrected from the initial baptism of death to your sin nature. This is made clear in the rest of Romans 6. Read alongside, as I try to explain the following verses:

Verse 5 tells you that you have been united with the resurrected Jesus Christ. You do not stay immersed into His death.

Verse 6 tells you that when you united with Christ, your old sin nature was dealt a fatal blow.

Verse 7 confirms your new freedom from the curse of your old sin nature.

Verse 8 tells you that you are not living on your own source now, but in the life (or living) of Jesus. You died with Christ and now you live by His life.

Verses 9 and 10 tell you that in Christ you no longer have the dominion of the sin nature controlling you, but now it is Christ's life that dominates you.

Now when you get to verse 11, Paul's emphatic statement is for you to **reckon yourselves to be dead indeed to sin, but alive to God in**

ಬು Transformed! ೧೩

Christ Jesus our Lord. This word, **reckon,** *logizomai,* means "to inventory, to take into account, to consider as done," to come to a logical conclusion—meaning, **it has happened.** Paul was flabbergasted at the way some "followers" were treating their conversion into Christianity. He was—and still is—telling his audience that genuine conversion was no less than a death to one life and a birth into another. To say that you are **born again** (John 3:3) is to say that you no longer live in the flesh's sinful dominant nature. You are now **alive to God in Christ Jesus our Lord** (6:11). You must **reckon** this. You must consider it as done—that you've had a spiritual baptism occur inside you and that the Spirit of the living God has now come inside you to live out the spiritual nature of the resurrected Christ.

As you continue reading Romans 6 (you are reading it, aren't you?), you will see in verse 15, and following, that Paul is asking if you **obeyed from the heart** (v. 17). **From the heart** means you have mentally, emotionally, and spiritually transformed your essence—your being—into the essence of Christ—that is, His righteousness (v. 18-20). This means you are now to **have your fruit to holiness** (v. 22). That means your wages in the resurrected life are now in the form of holiness, or Christ likeness. Previously, **the wages of sin** [was] **death** (v. 23), but now the wage has been replaced with **the gift of God** [which] **is eternal life in Christ Jesus our Lord** (v. 23). This replacement is explained in Romans 7 as a domination of ownership. Paul expresses it well as he relates it to his own personal struggle with the release of his Jewish indoctrination. It sounds as if it nearly killed him (7:13-25). Paul discovered that the final and full release of his fleshly bondage would not occur until his physical death or the return of Christ.

ஐ Baptism – A Symbol of Intimacy ௸

This explanation of baptism is a most difficult issue for a person to comprehend. To **die daily**, as Paul stated in 1 Corinthians 15:31, is a most tedious discipline for a born again follower of Jesus. Every new follower of Jesus experiences the new nature in a fresh and invigorating way at the onset of salvation. He has been immersed into a new nature. But then the flesh reminds this new nature that flesh is still around. The flesh is still the **outward man** and causes doubt of a new controlling source in the **inward man** (2 Cor. 4:16). The flesh impedes the growth of the spiritual nature. However, the Scriptures admonish the follower of Jesus to train to run his spiritual **race** to win (cf. 1 Cor. 9:24). He does this as he disciplines his body into spiritual subjection (1 Corinthians 9:24-27). The new nature is impeded by the mind of the flesh, called the **carnal mind** (Romans 8:7). This carnal (fleshly) mind has its residual resources from the old nature and is in direct opposition to the developing spiritual mind. The carnal mind is **death** (8:6) and must be overpowered by a transformed spiritual mind.

Most of Romans 8 details how to allow this spiritual mind to take first place. Then jumping to Romans 12 (chapters 9-11 appear to be a parenthetical issue where Paul deals with his fellow Jews), you will find the practical instruction on how to transform the carnal mind to a spiritual mind. Romans 12:1-2 gives you several steps for your spiritual baptism to result into a fruitful transformation. First, you must **present yourself** to God as **a living sacrifice**. As such, you forfeit all rights to your current existence. Notice, however, that this presentation is not to **death** as in the initial baptism for spiritual life. No, this presentation is into a **reasonable service** for God. You now allow Him to intervene in order to transform your mind for spiritual renewal, or reprogramming. This renewal allows you to **prove what is that good and acceptable and perfect will of God** (v. 2).

ೞ Transformed! ಐ

As spiritual transformation occurs, you begin to view the world from God's perspective. You begin to see your life as one of many members of the body of Christ, each serving faithfully, using the gift(s) God has given each for the betterment of all. This is explained in the rest of Romans, chapters 12-16. For example, **For none of us lives to himself, and no one dies to himself** (14:7). It is God who now wills your new nature. It is God who initiated your spiritual baptism; it is God who continues to transform you. Comprehend this and you will enjoy a tremendous life of service to God through Jesus Christ. And you will begin to experience spiritual power as the resource for your living.

Now take a moment and ask yourself a few serious questions: Does the above experience describe what has—or is—occurring in your life? Have you experienced a genuine spiritual baptism? That is, have you died to your self-control and been immersed into the Spirit of the living God? If so, where are you in the transformation? How much of your mind is renewed—God empowered? Prayerfully ask God and honestly answer the questions. If there are any areas of weaknesses revealed to you in prayer or from His Word, you need to stop serving in the flesh (carnal mind) and allow God's Spirit to renew your mind until the weaknesses are transformed. Perhaps now would be a good time to stop reading for a while to recharge your spiritual "batteries." Get alone with God for a while. Allow Him time to speak to you. Ask Him the above questions and let His Word invade your inner being with His answers. If you haven't done so, read prayerfully through Romans 12-16. These chapters offer great spiritual growth ideas.

---

* (Page 88) Greek grammar references are taken from The Complete Word Study New Testament With Parallel Greek, Spiros Zodhiates; AMG Publishers, Chattanooga, TN; 1992.

CHAPTER 4 ~ The Gift That Keeps Giving

Your baptism into Jesus Christ makes you a special gift to Him from God. In John 10:25-30, Jesus explained that He not only protected the gift He received from His Father, but His gift also enjoys a permanent shield of security by His and the Father's hands: **And I give them eternal life, and they shall never perish; neither shall anyone snatch them out of My hand. My Father, who has given them to Me, is greater than all; and no one is able to snatch them out of My Father's hand** (v. 28, 29).

The opening phrase above, **I give them**, is present active indicative in the Greek, meaning, something that is occurring while the speaker is making the statement. That assures the follower that **eternal life**—the shield of security—begins in the present tense. The **given** of verse 29 is in the perfect tense which, as explained earlier, means a completed task with continued results.

This shield of protection is described to be as secure as the oneness of Jesus with the Father (**I and My Father are one.** v. 30). What Jesus has done in this prayer request is to introduce His continuing oneness with the Father and with His followers. The **sheep** are one with Christ and are as secure in this oneness as is Jesus with the Father. Thus, the gift of God to Jesus' followers, which is eternal life in the Son (cf. Romans 6:23), is as secure as Jesus is with the Father. Now ask yourself this question: Can Jesus lose His eternal oneness with the Father? No, He cannot. If Jesus cannot, nor can His followers because they are an eternal gift of God given to Him. The only debatable exception may be Judas Iscariot. However, Jesus called Judas a **son of perdition** (John 17:12; cf. 2 Thessalonians 2:3), which indicates he was not a son of the Father or a genuine follower of Jesus. There can be Judas-acting "followers" still in the church today, so be sure your eternal security is based on God's Word and not on any man-produced or church-produced benefit.

God Among Sin?

Some well-meaning followers of Jesus Christ have a problem with the concept of eternal security because they do not think God will keep himself attached to a sinful person who keeps sinning even after a solid commitment to Jesus Christ has been made. Some may point to a Hebrews passage that says, **if we sin willfully after we have received the knowledge of the truth, there no longer remains a sacrifice for sins** (10:26). Also, another Hebrews passage says that

> **it is impossible for those who were once enlightened, and have tasted the heavenly gift, and have become partakers of the Holy Spirit, and have tasted the good word of God and the powers of the age to come, if they fall away, to renew them again to repentance, since they crucify again for themselves the Son of God, and put Him to an open shame** (6:4-6).

Both of these passages, however, speak to the **impossible** return to salvation. If salvation is not eternally secured and can be lost, **there no longer remains a sacrifice for sins** (10:26). That means there is no "Plan B" for salvation. If Hebrews 10:26 is referring to an apostate—one who may **have received**, that is, "to get hold of," **the knowledge of the truth**, but continues to **sin willfully** (present active participle), which is the fruit of rejection of Jesus Christ—then there is no other **sacrifice** [solution] **for sins**. Also, it is best to interpret Hebrews 6:4-6 as hypothetical (note the change of pronouns from **we** to **those, they**, and **them**). That means that if it were possible to lose one's salvation, **it is impossible...if they fall away, to renew them**

again... (6:4a, 6a). Once God baptizes the inner spirit of a person, **if** that person could break away from God's baptism, His word (above cited) says He cannot reenter. It is **impossible**.

There are no legitimate Christian groups or denominations that I know of that believe if a person can fall out of God's saving grace, that person can never return back. Those who believe you can "fall from grace" also believe you can return to His grace later on. But to believe this opens a deluge of problems concerning additional statements and symbols of the Bible used to define genuine salvation. The ability of a person to lose his salvation also weakens the biblical standard and symbol of marriage, baptism, and other spiritual teachings.

But how can God dwell within a man who may deliberately sin? This is difficult to answer, but the difficulty here is that the gift—a follower of Jesus—is trying to interpret and, therefore, think and act independently of the design and purpose of the Giver. The purpose of the gift is to be used by the recipient (Jesus) according to its design. What did Jesus say, in the above priestly prayer (John 17:20-26), is the purpose of His followers? If it had to be narrowed down, according to this passage, the purpose of the eternal keeping status of man is to manifest the eternal, inseparable glory of Jesus and the Father. Stated another way, according to the historical nature of God's manifested glory, the purpose of a follower of Jesus is to manifest—reveal—the glory of the eternal God. That's why another Scripture says that this **mystery which has been hidden from ages and from generations...now has been revealed to His saints...** [this mystery] **which is Christ in you, the hope of glory** (Colossians 1:26, 27). Christ **in you**, the hope of glory? That's what the Bible says; and that is the revealed **mystery** that has been hidden until Christ came.

ಬಿ TRANSFORMED! ଓଃ

You, as a follower of Jesus, are a gift from God to Jesus. But even more than that, the Bible says that you are a gift **of God** in Jesus. You're not just a present; you are a presence. Look at Romans 6:23, the second half, real carefully: **...but the gift *of God* is eternal life in Christ Jesus our Lord** (emphasis added). Paul explains in Second Corinthians that the blinding light of God's glory was shown in the face of Moses. Moses had to wear a veil over his face after meeting in the presence of God. But that veil is **taken away in Christ** (2 Cor.3:14; cf. v. 16). Therefore, if you are **in Christ**, the veiled glory of God's presence is in you.

Where's the Glory?

Years ago, a fast food company used several elderly ladies in a television commercial. They stood politely, staring at a beautiful hamburger bun, talking about how lovely the bun looked with all the hamburger trimmings. But something seemed amiss. Finally one of the ladies looks into the bun and cries out, "Where's the beef?" The commercial was braggadocios about the large hamburger patties found in this company's hamburgers.

Let's change the "product" a bit. There's a man next door to you who attends a church down the street regularly. He is married, has two children, and a stable job. He minds his own business and keeps his property clean. But one afternoon, police arrive at his home and arrest him for tax evasion. God looks into the man and says, "Where's the glory?"

Again, let's enlarge the "product." The church down the street from you is beautiful. It has a well-lit parking area and manicured landscaping. And lots of people attend the services. You decide to attend this church's services, but because you're of a different ethnicity, the usher shows you a seat in the balcony or a far corner. You receive stares as you find your seat. But God looks inside this beautiful church and cries out, "Where's the glory?"

Extreme examples? Maybe, or maybe not. Many so-called followers and many so-called Christian churches have a problem displaying the glorious presence of God. So what's the problem with the glory of God that is supposed to be manifested in

ೕ The Gift That Keeps Giving ಲ

followers? Why does it seem so veiled among followers today? And how may sin be allowed in God's presence? Perhaps the answer can be explained from another Scripture. Second Corinthians 4:6 commands this glory to shine out of a follower's heart (that is, his life); but verse seven explains the apparent difficulty: **But we have this treasure in earthen vessels, that the excellence of the power may be of God and not of us.** Simply stated, God's glory in man will not—cannot—be manifested **in** man's flesh, but **within** his flesh. Remember, that's where the spiritual transformation occurs. The **gift of God** is your baptism of eternal life in Jesus Christ. It is a life where the glory of God can reside. This is why the Bible consistently says that your body is the temple of God and is the place where God resides (John 14:23; 1 Corinthians 6:19-20; 2 Corinthians 6:16).

Here's another example: In the Old Covenant dispensation, was it the Jewish temple itself that revealed the glory of God, or was it His presence in the temple that revealed His glorious presence? It was His presence. And this is still the same in the New Covenant through Jesus Christ. Just as the Jewish temple wore out and was even destroyed at certain periods of time, so the New Covenant's "temple"—your body—is capable of wearing out. The glory of God is not in your flesh (the **outward man**, 2 Corinthians 4:16), but within your flesh (the **inward man**, 4:16). The glory must reveal itself through the perishing nature of the flesh. But what attribute is it that allows the glory to reveal itself? What attribute in man can empower the revelation of God's glory? Read 2 Corinthians 4:16-18 carefully for the answer:

> **Therefore we do not lose heart. Even though our outward man is perishing, yet the inward man is being renewed day by day. For our light affliction, which is for a moment, is working for us a far more exceeding and eternal weight of glory, while we do not look at the things which are seen, but at the things which are not seen. For the things which are seen are temporary, but the things which are not seen are eternal.**

Is not the **day by day** renewal of **faith** the attribute described here that allows the glory of God to be revealed in the inner man? Although the word "faith" is not found in the above passage, it is implied twice in the passage as **things which are not seen** (v. 18; cf. Hebrews 11:1), and is described as the channel of the revealed glory of God. Faith is the way the inner glory gets manifested in the flesh. Although it may be painful and burdensome in the flesh (2 Corinthians 5:1-4), it is still your command to **walk by faith, not by sight** (2 Corinthians 5:7). Yet, in the flesh, you must fight your physical nature that naturally wants to suppress living by faith. This is the battleground of the glory of God within you. The Spirit of God, in your spirit, must fight to discipline and dominate your natural soul's senses in your flesh, in order for the glory within to be revealed (unveiled) by faith. Does this make sense? Let me illustrate.

On numerous occasions, Jesus asked His followers to act on His commands in faith. He told them to feed thousands of people from one lad's lunch (John 6:5ff). He also stated that if they had only a mustard-seed size of faith, they could move a mountain (Matthew 17:20). On one occasion, Jesus had one of His followers walking on water toward Him (Matthew 14:25ff). This list could continue, but the point of these illustrations is that the flesh will argue against living by and acting in faith. In the flesh, obeying the words of Jesus may appear risky and sometimes absurd. However, the faith-life of a follower of Jesus is the key that unveils the glory—the gift—of God in you. God commands that the life of Jesus continue to be **manifested in** [your] **mortal flesh** (2 Corinthians 4:11). This is the purpose of the eternal gift in you. This is the purpose of your life on earth: to **walk by faith**. Let's walk a little deeper into the biblical concept of a faith-life.

CHAPTER 5 ~ Now Faith Is...

Now faith is the substance of things hoped for, the evidence of things not seen. For by it the elders obtained a good testimony. –Hebrews 11:1-2

The simple statement of Hebrews 11:1-2 reveals the salvation of all believers under God's chain of covenants on both sides of the cross of Jesus Christ. It would do you well to study this statement carefully. Let's dissect it a bit in its original language.

Faith in the Greek language is *pistis*, which means, "reliance, confidence, belief, or conviction of (religious) truth." The same word is used in the verse just above Hebrews 11:1, but is translated as **believe** (10:39). Add to faith the word **substance**. Substance is *hupostasis*, from *hupo*, which means, "under, beneath, or support," and *stasis*, which means, "(to) stand, abide, or set up." Together, you get the definition of **substance** as a mental, spiritual, and (sometimes) physical foundation (understanding) on which to stop or stand upon. It is the essence of being. Faith, then, becomes your mental and moral conviction by which your spiritual beliefs are founded upon and stand.

In Hebrews 1:3 you'll find this same Greek word translated as **person**, referring to Jesus as **the brightness of** [God's] **glory and the express image of His person** (*hupostasis*). This means Jesus is the substance—the personhood—of God. Faith is the substance—the essence—of a follower's spiritual being. It is the foundational means of understanding and relating to God and all spirituality. As substance, faith is as real to the follower of Jesus as Jesus is the personhood of God. Christianity is founded upon Jesus as God in flesh. Does your faith believe that? Is your faith's substance as strong as this belief? Would someone describe your spiritual life as a man or woman of faith? **Now faith is the substance…**

Next, add the phrase, **of things hoped for**. It is one word in Greek: *elpizomenon*. Many followers of Jesus misunderstand this word phrase. They may define this phrase as wishful thinking: These are the things I "hope" to get for Christmas. Thus faith, to them, is a hopeful conclusion of something asked for or desired. However, the Greek word is a compound word: *el*—from Hebrew origin, meaning, "strength, mighty," and is the syllable in Hebrew and Greek words to introduce God as Almighty; and *pizomenon* is from *pistis* (faith). Together, it means, "to have a strong belief in the reality of God." You can translate this introductory phrase in Hebrews 11:1 as such: *"Now faith is the foundation of the reality of God;"* or whittle it down some to: *"Now faith is founded upon the reality of God;"* or, still a bit further to: *"Now faith is the reality God."* Let that sink in for a moment.

God is the originator and substance (or essence) of faith; He is the understanding, foundation, and reality of faith. As such, He is **the evidence of things not seen**. The word **evidence**, has another *el* opening syllable: *elegchos*, meaning, "(strong) proof, conviction." It is a legal term meaning, "an item or testimony that leads to a conviction." It is evidence that leaves no question unanswered.

So faith originates in God because God is its foundation; He's the convicting (strong, assured, real) proof—the evidence—of your faith and in all spiritual things because He is in you. Therefore, you can stand strong in your faith because you are not standing alone. God stands with you. That (or He) is the evidence of your faith.

Did you get all that in? Look at the verse again with the Greek on top and English underneath. Look at it carefully:

ೂ Now Faith Is... ಡ

Pistis = *hupostasis* + *elpizomenon* + *elegchos*
Faith = the <u>foundation</u> of + the <u>reality of God</u> + the <u>evidence of God</u>

Now faith is the <u>substance</u> of <u>things hoped for</u>, the <u>evidence of things not seen</u>. (NKJV)

Putting the above verse in reverse order, the evidence of God, the reality of God, and the substance (the foundation) of God is faith. And, more specifically, the combined evidence, reality, and foundation of God in you **are the substances of your faith**. Your faith is the channel from which spiritual transformation occurs. Faith—active faith—is a follower's spiritual lifeblood. Habakkuk 2:4 says: **The just shall live by his faith.** This verse is quoted three more times in the New Testament (Romans 1:17, Galatians 3:11, and Hebrews 10:38), so it must be very important to God for you to understand this concept.

Many followers fail to comprehend what genuine faith is. This is why the concept of faith is defined in such varied ways among Christian groups. Some say faith is a verb—something you do or say; others say it is a noun—something that is done or is tangible...it is both! Some say faith is receiving; others say faith is giving...it is both! It is important that you allow faith to be the essence—the reality—of God in you. You act in faith because faith is your life within the confines of the living presence of God within you. Faith is allowing God to move you from within. This takes you back to the end of the last chapter, where you were commanded to **walk by faith, not by sight** (2 Corinthians 5:7). This command is to simply live under the confident control of God's Spirit within you. This is how the glory of God (**the gift of God** –Romans 6:23) in you gets out of you. You must walk and live by faith. This is your testimony of the reality of God in you. This is the same testimony of the **elders**, mentioned in Hebrews 11:2. They lived their entire lives before God in the faith of His word that He would bring a Redeemer to restore mankind to its original design. There are many testimonies of living by faith given in Hebrews, chapter eleven. Let's read about one in particular.

Abraham's Faith and Failure

Abram—later called, Abraham—believed he received a word from God to leave his country, his kindred, and therefore his future inheritance, to travel to a faraway **land of promise** (Hebrews 11:9). He left with his immediate family, a few relatives, and some animals to uncharted territory that God said would become his (Genesis 12:1-8).

When Abram arrived, there was no welcoming committee from the locals. He fought for a place in which to pitch his tents and he fought a famine that was waiting for him. He did not establish a town and call it Abramville. God assured him that a utopia would be created for his descendents. Therefore, he turned and kept his attention on the establishment of his descendents. Since they had no children, to believe God's promise would be the highest test of faith in his walk with and belief in the God who spoke to him. As you read through the story of Abraham, you will find him in situations where he failed to act in faith with his God (cf., Genesis 12:10-20; 16:1-6; 20:1-16). However, these incidences are written to show God's faithfulness to work through the unfaithfulness of His children. There's a lesson in this for all followers.

Though Abraham failed, God kept His promise with Abraham because, by and large, he was faithful. God promised him a child by faith: Isaac would be his name (Genesis 17:15-19). But prior to this child of faith, Abraham and Sarah tried to provide descendents through their own fleshly activity outside of faith in God. Thus Ishmael was born (Genesis 16:1-6). Abraham received tremendous trouble because He failed in the flesh. He failed to understand that God's restoration of mankind was never intended to be through the fleshly means of a fallen human nature. It would be and continues to be by promise and by faith.

ೞ Now Faith Is... ೲ

Something Less Than Faith to Control You

Let us return to an application of the definition of faith. God's glory is revealed by faith. But faith is not faith if you have to see it first or if you can manipulate it. And many times faith is not even understandable. Faith can be seen and it can be understood, but only through the eyes and mind of God. This is how the **elders** obtained **a good testimony** (Hebrews 11:2); that is, they gave and lived by an honest report, testifying of the reality of a living God. Faith is testifying that there is a real living God inside you, leading and controlling you. Anything less is simply a dependency on your soul-controlled, fleshly nature. This is how the glory of God is revealed. It will not be revealed in your flesh, but through your flesh. What does this mean and how is this fleshed out?

The fleshly nature of a person is founded on the basic primary senses: sight, hearing, touch, taste, and smell. The mind and body can take these five senses and produce unusual qualities in a person. Behavior, reason, intellect, and intuition are such qualities formulated from man's soul senses. Everyone has a soul regardless of his or her religious affiliation, atheists included. Becoming a follower of Jesus Christ does not alter the soul's senses in any form or fashion. As stated in a previous chapter, God comes into the soul of a person and revives it by the birth of a spirit; that is, He brings man's spirit back to life. The human spirit, previously dead to a God-consciousness, now becomes invigorated (resurrected) with the life of God. The Spirit of God invades your soul for the express purpose of controlling its senses for the purpose of God. The transfer of soul-control takes time and much discipline, and can only be accomplished by the discipline of faith. You must, by faith, release control of your senses to Him. This release does not mean that you begin performing less as a human; rather, it means that you will begin to add a new spiritual dimension (a sixth sense?) to your performance, under the guidance of the Holy Spirit. The Spirit-controlled soul of a man will burst forth in an enormous amount of ministry for God. This ministry is His glory—this ministry is Jesus' ministry being manifested on the earth once again. **By this is My Father glorified, that you bear much fruit; so you will be My disciples**

(John 15:8; cf. John 15:16). As a disciple, you continue the spiritual teaching and ministry of Jesus and you will **bear much fruit**.

Now the question is, do you have faith to believe this? Let me illustrate. If, while meditating on God's Word about a missionary journey of Paul, God impresses upon your spirit to follow Him into a mission ministry, will you begin preparations to do it? If, while you are praying, God speaks an answer to your prayer, will you begin to thank Him for the answer immediately? If God gives you direction in your life through a sermon or a song, will you obey His directive?

Remember an important thing about a life of faith: it will not contradict the personhood of God, because faith is the **substance**, the **evidence**, and the **testimony** of God (Hebrews 11:1-2). A life of faith will not be a chaotic life, for God's presence is a presence of **love, joy, peace, patience, kindness, goodness, faithfulness, gentleness,** and **self-control** (cf. Galatians 5:22-23). He will not lead you to contradict Himself. A life of faith exemplifies God's nature. A life of faith pleases God, for **without faith it is impossible to please Him, for he who comes to God must believe that He is, and that He is a rewarder of those who diligently seek Him** (Hebrews 11:6). Notice the qualifying word, **diligence**. God rewards those who are diligent in their faith. Be diligent in your faith in God and watch the glory of God be manifested in you and flow through you. The glory of God is the follower's life, under the control of the Holy Spirit, and is the substance of his faith. Comprehend this and you will go far in the process of spiritual transformation.

CHAPTER 6 ~ Am I Worth a Million Bucks or What?!

The peace of God inside you and a life-walk of faith are invaluable and inseparable. When you allow the Spirit of God to control you, you will then begin to understand more of the nature and purpose of God. One very important revelation God will give you in your life-walk of faith is your eternality in God. It begins with eternity past:

For whom He foreknew, He also predestined to be conformed to the image of His Son, that He might be the firstborn among many brethren. Moreover whom He predestined, these He also called; whom He called, these He also justified; and whom He justified, these He also glorified.
–Romans 8:29-30

You have a past. God **foreknew** you. The greatest hindrance to the future of a follower of Jesus Christ is his inability to see his past from God's perspective. So many Christians live in the present. This affects their ability to walk in faith because they are seeking a present life of recognition, happiness, pleasure, or a variety of other soul-initiated vices. This is a form of Christian hedonism and is contrary to all biblical directives for a usable follower.

Your present life has the purpose of revealing the glory of God. To do that, you must understand your beginning with Him. We'll do that by evaluating the above verses of Romans. The word, **foreknew** (or **foreknowledge**) tells you that God knew you beforehand—He knew you before you knew Him. Because of His knowledge of you before you were a you, He has allowed you to become who you are, where you are, with what you are. Huh? Hang on; it gets a little more complicated.

The next phrase in the above verses says that God **predestined** you. The word in Greek is *prohoridzo*. The prefix *pro-* means "in front of, prior or superior to," and is used with *horidzo*, which means, "to map out with a boundary, to be appointed, to decree or specify" (English: horizon). To be **predestined** by God simply means that He has pre-established you within your physical boundaries for an eternal purpose. What is your predestined eternal purpose? Look at the next phrase: **to be conformed to the image of His Son. Conformed** has two primary meanings in the Greek. One is *suschematizo*, from *sūn*, meaning, "to form a union by association, companionship, resemblance, etc.," and, *schema*, meaning, "an external figure or condition" (English: schematic). You'll find this rendering of **conformed** in Romans 12:2: **And do not be conformed to this world...** that is, do not fashion your new union with God according to the drawings (schematics) of your physical and/or natural surroundings—your existing culture or era.

The other meaning of **conformed**, as found in our current passage (Romans 8:29), is *summorphos*, from *sūn* (see above definition) and *morphe*, meaning, "the adjustment of shape or nature." Apply this meaning to Romans 8:29 and you get the idea that you have been eternally predestined to form a new nature of Christ likeness through an inner spiritual union with Him. This takes you back to your identity with the Son of God. He is called **the firstborn among many brethren** (v. 29). What does this say to you?

ཨ AM I WORTH A MILLION BUCKS OR WHAT?! ༀ

If the Scriptures say that you are to conform your new nature to the image (likeness) of Jesus, how can you live physically in this likeness? The key is in the remainder of the Romans verses above. First note the word, **called**. The Greek word means, "to be summoned with the idea of an appointment or vocation." God sets you up with an appointment to walk in the likeness of Jesus. He does this through your flesh by His declaration of you becoming **justified** and **glorified**. **Justified** means, "to be declared just, righteous, and/or free." **Glorified** means, "to render or esteem as glorious." Positionally speaking, this means that God has **called** you out of your previous location of darkness and has reestablished you in a place of honor, brilliance, and magnanimity. Again, remember that this is not being done to your flesh and its nature over your soul, but to that which He has birthed into you when His Spirit entered you.

Also, it will be very helpful for you to know that the above words (**foreknew, predestined, called, justified,** and **glorified**) are all, in the Greek, aorist indicative active, meaning that all this is seen from God's eternal perspective (past, present, and future) as a completed declaration that occurred at a follower's conversion, and is continuing to occur until the reuniting of the follower with Jesus Christ is completed, either at his death or when the return of Christ occurs. When Jesus went through the process of His death, burial, and resurrection, He experienced a conversion. He experienced the **baptism into death** (Romans 6:4). His death surrendered His ability to operate physically. His burial showed that what He was to become, for the glory of God, would not be through His temporary physical nature. And His resurrection showed that His new life would be solely at the call, mercy, and power of God.

The Beat Goes On

If the ministry of Jesus had been completed in the act of His resurrection, His followers would have been left in confusion as to how to act through their physical lives while awaiting His return or their deaths. What you find, however, is an important portion of Scripture that presents Jesus in His new physical/spiritual nature.

☙ Transformed! ❧

The life of the new resurrected Jesus presents an outline for all His followers.

Jesus spent forty days before His followers in a resurrected state of existence, teaching and revealing a new lifestyle to His followers. His forty days may be symbolic of our life (a generation?) here on earth. It behooves you to read and understand His resurrected lifestyle carefully. Let's take a look.

CHAPTER 7 ~ Forty Days That Changed the World

Jesus spent forty days on the earth after He was resurrected (Acts 1:3). Portions of the events of the post-grave, resurrected life of Jesus can be found in all four gospels and in the book of Acts. It is not the intent of this chapter to expound everything Jesus said and did after He arose from the grave, but to give you an outline as to His essence and purpose as a resurrected, **firstborn among many brethren** (Romans 8:29). To follow Jesus' calling is not to mimic Him verbatim, but to exemplify Him in His essence and purpose for those forty days He spent with His followers.

Source of Life and Spiritual Understanding

The very first thing all the passages teach is that Jesus received life after death. God raised up Jesus from His tomb. Paul says that

> **He rose again the third day according to the Scriptures, and that He was seen by Cephas** [Peter], **then by the twelve. After that He was seen by over five hundred brethren at once, of whom the greater part remain to the present** [Paul's generation], **but some have fallen asleep. After that He was seen by James, then by all the apostles. Then last of all He was seen by me also, as by one born out of due time** (1 Corinthians 15:4b-8).

ಲು Transformed! ಬ

All the eyewitness accounts of the resurrected Jesus led to an incredible sweep of Christianity through the civilized world, making it impossible to stop.

This becomes the foundation of all that occurred during that forty-day period. Jesus was alive—both physically and spiritually. He ate, He talked, He walked, and He reasoned among His followers. He was seen by hundreds of people. He gave a commission to all His followers to go and do what He had been doing among them. This "Great Commission" is found in all the gospels and the book of Acts (Matthew 28:18-20; Mark 16:15-18; Luke 24:46-49; John 20:21-23; Acts 1:7-8). Every follower of Jesus has been commissioned to exemplify the resurrected Christ in proclaiming His message. The Great Commission is the marching orders for every follower.

But the resurrected Christ did more than just give His followers marching orders. Jesus taught them during that forty-day period. It says that He opened their eyes to see Him (Luke 24:31) and that **He opened their understanding, that they might comprehend the Scriptures** (Luke 24:45). Thus, a follower of Jesus is one who is diligent to open and understand the Scriptures and to see Christ in His essence.

Supplies All Needs

Another thing Jesus did during the forty days was to go to the job site of Peter, John, and a few others (John 21:1-25). He did this to show that He was Lord over a follower's occupation. This fact is very difficult for many followers to comprehend and/or accept. Many followers think their purpose in life is primarily to work, earn a living, provide for their families, and, as time allows, go to church. But this thinking is a natural soul-originated one; it is centered around man's purpose, as he perceives life, and not God's purpose, as the Scriptures teach. Had Jesus not showed up at the job site and had not His followers yielded to Him, they would have had a fruitless night of fishing:

But when the morning had come, Jesus stood on the shore; yet the disciples did not know that it was Jesus. Then He said to them, "Children, have you any food?" They answered Him, "No." And He said to them, "Cast the net on the right side of the boat, and you will find some." So they cast, and now they were not able to draw it in because of the multitude of fish. Therefore that disciple whom Jesus loved said to Peter, "It is the Lord!" –John 21:4-7a

It is interesting to note that in this story, when the disciples brought in their catch, Jesus already had a fire of coals going with fish laid on it and bread—enough, as He had proven beforehand, to feed thousands of people (v. 9; cf. Matthew 14:17-21). This was—and still is—His way of showing that He was the supply for all their needs, both physical and spiritual. Jesus wants you to trust Him on the job. The purpose of your job is to manifest the glory of God in you while you enjoy the job.

Restoring Personal Faith

Another thing Jesus did during the above episode was to restore the usefulness and faith of Peter. Peter had denied his Lord three times during the trials of Jesus. After eating the fish, you hear Jesus (three times, no doubt) telling Peter to get back into the business of shepherding people. Jesus called Peter to catch people, not fish. The lesson here is the nature of forgiveness permeating Jesus' resurrected life and for His followers to remain focused on their calling. **Peter, seeing [John], said to Jesus, But Lord, what about this man?" Jesus said to him, "If I will that he remain till I come, what is that to you? You follow me."** –John 21:21-22 (cf., Matt. 18:21-22) Jesus forgave Peter and restored his personal calling to shepherd God's people. When forgiving others who have wronged you becomes your nature, this attitude allows you to remain focused on your calling to manifest His glory in you.

∞ Transformed! ∞

Fellowship

Another thing Jesus did was to have fellowship with His followers. He ate with them, prayed with them, and blessed their gathering. Fellowship should be a time for joyful and celebrated expressions. It should be a time to pray for one another. According to Jude, verse 12, the early followers of Jesus participated in agape (love) feasts, which involved a fellowship meal for all and a time of sharing Godly care and concern for one another. Paul also alluded to these feasts when he rebuked the Corinthian church for abusing the Lord's Supper during the feast by segregating the people into culture classes (1 Corinthians 11:17-22). Although both of these references are presented negatively in their context, it was never the intent of the writers to tell the church to stop having fellowships. Fellowships should be encouraged among His followers.

Worship

Jesus also allowed His followers to worship Him and to call Him their **Lord and** [their] **God** (John 20:28). Volumes have been written on the nature and command to worship Jesus Christ as the Almighty God. This is a great priority and should be a natural part of a follower's daily life. In brief, worship is adoration and honor given to God through Jesus Christ. Worship involves fellowship, exhortation (encouragement), praise, prayer, singing, and/or proclamation of His Word. Worship is both a public and private display of submission to the essence and purpose of God in a follower's life. Worship can be lively or it can be a period of silence. It can be with a body of followers or in sweet solitude.

Power

During the forty days of the resurrected Jesus, He also displayed enormous power and control over natural elements on the earth. This statement may send up a spiritual "red flag" among some who read this, but it is still a written truth. The problem of abuse causes the red flag. Therefore be careful in this area, because, once again, the essence and purpose of Christ in you is to reveal the spiritual side of life. If you will read Mark 16:17-18, you will find some interesting **signs** that **will follow those who believe.** Many Bible versions will contain a marginal note that will tell you that these verses are questionable insertions, meaning that perhaps they were not in the original writings of Mark's gospel. The fact remains, however that they are found in many of the early Greek fragments of Mark. Let's therefore assume they are valid verses. What do you make of them?

The best—and, I believe, the safest—way is to attribute these **signs** as those that accompanied the early followers as a source of validation to their new message. The Scriptures repeatedly confirm these signs as a part of the early ministry of the apostles, thus called apostolic sign gifts. As the first century wound down and the first generation of Jesus' followers passed away, the writings of the second generation of Christians explain that many of these sign gifts became less and less identifiable and necessary as the canon of Scripture was being formed. That canon became known as the New Covenant of God, now called the New Testament, as found in Christian Bibles. Again, just as with worship, many volumes have been written on the subject of apostolic sign gifts and you can spend countless dollars and hours reading on the subject…but not in this volume.*

To summarize, Jesus spent His resurrected life on this earth, 1.) to display victory over death, 2.) to commission His followers to go and tell of this new life in Christ, 3.) to teach and comprehend the Scriptures, 4.) to worship Jesus Christ as God, 5.) to trust Him fully to meet all a follower's needs, 6.) to display a forgiving spirit in order to help restore people back into the purpose of God for their lives, 7.) to fellowship with other believers, and 8.) to recognize the power of Christ over the earth:

All authority has been given to Me in heaven and on earth. Go therefore and make disciples of all the nations, baptizing them in the name of the Father and of the Son and of the Holy Spirit, teaching them to observe all things that I have commanded you; and lo, I am with you always, even to the end of the age (Matthew 28:18-19a).

ও Transformed! ଓଃ

But there is one more important thing to know that Jesus said for all followers to do as a resurrected being: **Behold, I send the Promise of My Father upon you; but tarry in the city of Jerusalem until you are endued with power from on high** (Luke 24:49). Before you can go, before you can baptize, before you can teach, before you can even worship effectively, or any of the things mentioned above, you must have the power of the **Promise of My Father upon you**. This is a reference to the presence of the indwelling Holy Spirit of God. Jesus had taught His followers previously that **without Me you can do nothing** (John 15:5c). And He is explaining this right in the middle of His assurance that He would indeed send to His followers the Holy Spirit to indwell them (cf. John 14-17). This is added assurance that you cannot live the Christian life apart from the living Christ. Therefore, 9.) you must learn to wait (**tarry**) on the Spirit; He must **endue** you with the spiritual power necessary to reveal Christ in and through you. This is the **hope of glory** (Colossians 1:27); this is the way the glory is revealed in you and through you.

Again, it is not a fleshly thing; it is not a display of a souped-up soul. Jesus was still Jesus in His fleshly manifestation during those forty days. He still had His scars from His crucifixion and He still put food into His mouth. But Jesus now operated in a new sphere of reality. He was the power of God in His resurrected flesh. This same power is the presence of God's Spirit dwelling in your spirit and manifesting Himself through you. This power does not alter your flesh and it doesn't even alter your soul. It certainly can light a fire in your emotions, but there is no standard set in the Scriptures as to how you will respond to the emanating power of the Holy Spirit in and through you, other than humility. According to your God-given temperament, you will sense God's presence in your life. Your flesh and your soul will be as normal as they have always been—no, actually, they will be more normal than ever.

This is how every follower of Jesus Christ should act and live. This is the outline of your resurrected life according to the example of Jesus. You must **tarry** with your Lord to discover how His will fits into your everyday lifestyle. In the first chapter of PART TWO, you were told to wait for God to speak. Jesus placed a high priority on waiting for His Father to speak. He prayed often and told His followers to do the same. No follower is commissioned to do anything without the accompanying spiritual power to energize the revelation of Jesus Christ in what he does. To do otherwise is spiritual hypocrisy and produces a counterfeit Christianity. Too much preaching, teaching, and other "spiritual" deeds already exist without the power of the Spirit invested in them. A flesh-driven, soul-powered ministry is why many followers remain powerless to affect their families, churches, and communities for Christ. They would rather do something than admit that **the glory has departed** (1 Samuel 4:21). Members of the evangelical church of today must return to the revealed Word of God to rediscover their spiritual roots and reclaim its power. The early followers spread Christianity rapidly through the civilized world because they waited for the glorious power of God to come upon them. This can happen again as followers today rediscover how to wait for and act in the spiritual power of a resurrected life.

The purpose of PART TWO of this book is to get you, as a follower, to transform your natural soul nature to a Spirit-controlled, Spirit-dominated soul nature. If you have an inkling of a desire to become this type of follower, I counsel you to jot the above-mentioned nine things down and to rehearse them with the Scriptures given and with other verses found in your Bible. Then, on your knees (or as you're able), pour your heart out before God in prayer as you pour through His Word for direction and correction. **Wait on the Lord; be of good courage, and He shall strengthen your heart; wait, I say, on the Lord!** (Psalm 27:14) This Psalm is a good place to start in your quietness before God. Try it.

---

* (Page 115) I do not discount all extraordinary manifestations of spiritual gifts as extra-biblical. If the written Word of God, in conjunction with the Holy Spirit, cannot be used to validate the gospel of Jesus Christ today, say, for example, in a foreign land where there may be a language barrier, God's Spirit certainly has the option of validating His message as He sees fit. I know

☙ TRANSFORMED! ☙

---

this statement may open a deluge of questions, but I have the personal conviction that God still has a few prerogatives of His own.

Having said this, I also know that God's Word has a few restrictions and guidelines for the purpose of validating His message. I would question any use of an apostolic sign gift that brought attention to a person or group, rather than to the Person of Jesus Christ—or to the human messenger, rather than the heavenly message.

CHAPTER 8 ~ Why is God in Me?

There's an important word in the New Testament that helps explain the movement of God in the process of transforming a follower of Jesus. Comprehend this word and its impact to your spiritual transformation, and it will increase your awareness of God's presence. Let's read a couple verses of Scripture with this important word and then dissect it.

> **Much more then, having now been justified by His blood, we shall be saved from wrath through Him. For if when we were enemies we were *reconciled* to God through the death of His Son, much more, having been *reconciled*, we shall be saved by His life.** –Romans 5:9-10 (emphasis added).
>
> **Therefore, if anyone is in Christ, he is a new creation; old things have passed away; behold, all things have become new. Now all things are of God, who has *reconciled* us to Himself through Jesus Christ, and has given us the ministry of *reconciliation*...Now then, we are ambassadors for Christ, as though God were pleading through us: we implore you on Christ's behalf, be *reconciled* to God.** –2 Corinthians 5:17-18, 20 (emphasis added)

Reconciled and **reconciliation** are active words. They describe what God does to you when He enters you and what He wants you to help others do with Him. In the Greek, the word is *katallasso*, from *kata*, meaning, "to come down upon" (usually with intensity), and *allasso*, meaning, "to make different, to change" (English: alias). Thus, God is in the business of changing people. He does that by coming "down upon" them (just as He did to you) and entering into them by His Spirit. When the Spirit of God enters a person, that person changes; his nature is altered when reconciliation occurs.

God always initiates the change between Himself and others. But He has given you a **ministry of reconciliation**. This ministry is bringing others into a position of understanding what God desires of them. And His desire for man is to receive the living Spirit of God into their inner being and be reconciled to Him. You cannot perform the actual act of reconciliation, but God has chosen you, as His ambassador, to make contact with those who are outside His commonwealth and to align them for the spiritual reception of reconciliation. This is your **ministry of reconciliation**.

Rejected

Let's look at the big picture for a moment. God has promised one more face-to-face encounter with every human, whether they are saved (in Christ) or lost (outside of Christ). When the encounter occurs, eternal change occurs. There will be an evaluation performed on all people individually. For those without the Spirit of Christ dwelling in them, they will be assigned an everlasting place of separation from God and be tormented in a place called hell (cf., Revelation 20:7-15; Luke 16:19-31). This is the dangerous part of *katallasso* and is referred to as the **second death** (Revelation 2:11; 20:6, 14). Being brought into God's presence without the blood of Christ to cover a person's sin nature means eternal death for that person. Why? Because such a person has previously rejected God's offer to be reconciled through the blood sacrifice of Jesus Christ. He has refused to allow God to come into his inner being and, therefore, has lost all opportunities for reconsideration.

Redeemed

For those who already have the Spirit of Christ dwelling in them, they will be positioned at a separate evaluation place and each person will be judged for all deeds performed as a follower of Jesus. This will be a time of rewards and a welcome into a dwelling place, called heaven, prepared by Jesus Himself (John 14:1-4). These individuals have received God's offer to unite with Him through Christ and are, therefore, redeemed.

There is a big difference in the two indeed. Understand the enormity of the difference and you will understand the importance of getting more involved in the **ministry of reconciliation**. You will also understand why Jesus had to shed His blood for this **reconciled** encounter. God cannot approach man's presence without a blood sacrifice to atone for sins. Jesus' sacrifice allows any person who has been atoned by His blood into the presence of Almighty God without the fear of judgment. When God approaches a follower of Jesus, He sees the blood of Christ "sprinkled" on him and declares him righteous (**justified**).

The **ministry of reconciliation** is intercepting this encounter, on man's behalf, and **pleading**, on God's behalf, for man to receive the blood sacrifice before the actual encounter occurs. It's similar to what an attorney may try to do for a client before an actual trial occurs. He may try to "plea bargain" or "settle" out of court for a client for fear of the sentencing that may come from the judge or a jury. The difference in the spiritual settlement is that once the face-to-face encounter occurs there are no further deliberations and no settlements to make. Once an individual's physical death occurs or once the "trumpet" announcement of Jesus' return to earth occurs, all "decision" opportunities are ended; the **ministry of reconciliation** is over: **...it is appointed for men to die once, but after this the judgment** (Hebrews 9:27). This is the big picture of God's plan for all mankind.

Now back to you, the follower of Jesus: to be **reconciled** means you are the recipient of God's Spirit. In reconciliation, God is restoring you back to His original intent for you. You are now free to walk in calm assurance of the protective presence of Almighty God. In you, God's Spirit begins to restore all the spiritual qualities that prepare you for a special union with His Son, called the marriage supper of the Lamb (Revelation 19:5-9). You are to be adorned as the bride for the greatest marriage for all eternity. This is to be the greatest celebration of mankind with His Creator since His creation of the first man and woman. This wedding will restore the intended union between God and man. Together, as joint heirs, you and Christ will enjoy all the inheritance reserved for the Son and His bride, the church. In fact, Jesus says He is preparing a dwelling place for His bride, **that where I am, there you may be also** (John 14:3b). This will be the time when the consummation of the eternal relationship occurs for all believers.

But before you go into the "marriage" relationship with Christ and God, there are a number of things you must first work into your current "betrothal" relationship. Plus there are still a few things He wants you to do and experience here on the earth as an instrument of His bigger plan.

For I have betrothed you to one husband, that I may present you as a chaste virgin to Christ (2 Cor. 11:2-3). Paul understood his ministry of reconciliation. He knew that every person to whom he led to Christ would join the universal, eternal church of promise, **as a chaste virgin to Christ**. This is the description that the Holy Spirit employed on the church—every follower of Christ.

Throughout the Old Testament, a betrothed virgin was protected by God. Any man (or the betrothed virgin) who violated the betrothal would be put to death (cf.: Deuteronomy 22:23-29). This command of God was followed by the Jews into the New Testament era (cf.: Matthew 1:18-19). The man to whom the betrothed virgin would marry, worked to prepare for her redemption (Leviticus 19:20).

Today we know that Christ is now preparing a place for His betrothed bride, the church. He has fulfilled all the law of God and is gone to heaven now to prepare for the arrival of His bride. The redemption plan is complete, awaiting only the fulfillment of the numerical size of the bride. The age-old question is when will the numerical size of the bride be complete? Only the Father and the Son know.

Meanwhile, the followers of Christ should be acting as a part of the betrothed virgin. And they should also be excited to tell others of this betrothal and the invitation of the Husband to join into the bride. This is your **ministry of reconciliation**; this is a part of your priestly function: to intercede on behalf of man to be reconciled to God. The Scripture says you have become: a priest in a holy and royal priesthood. Let's look carefully at your role as a priest in this reconciling ministry.

ಬ Transformed! ೞ

CHAPTER 9 ~ The Priesthood of Man

Therefore, in all things He had to be made like His brethren, that He might be a merciful and faithful High Priest in things pertaining to God, to make propitiation for the sins of the people. –Hebrews 2:17

As a spiritual ambassador in the ministry of reconciliation, you must undergo certain preparations and qualifications before the work can be performed through you. There are still some people who need to be introduced to God's redemptive plan. God says that you, who are already a part of the bride, must follow the steps of Jesus and become a priest in your mediatory role and negotiating performance in behalf of mankind.

The word priest in Greek is *heiroos*, from *heiros*, meaning, "holy, sacred, and divine." *Heiroos* is defined as "one who participates in holy, sacred, and/or divine things;" it is one who mediates between two in an agreement with one another. *Heiroos* focuses primarily on the external functions of a priest.

As we have seen in a previous chapter (Chapter 2 of PART TWO), Jesus is called a High Priest in the Bible. Let's look at some of the priestly functions of Jesus. In Hebrews 2:17, Jesus mediated first **to make propitiation for the sins of the people.** Propitiation is a word that needs careful explanation. In Greek it is *hilasmos*, which means, "to appease or conciliate" (gain favor). This word is best understood by its Old Testament Hebrew equivalent, *kaphar*, which basically means, "to cover." Its meaning is expanded to mean, "to cleanse, disannul, forgive, pacify, pardon, or purge." To propitiate means to cover sin as an act of mercy from God.

In the Old Testament, God's wrath against sin was propitiated (appeased) by a system of sacrifices. Animal blood was used to "cover" the sins of God's people. Leviticus, chapters 16 and 17, gives a few examples of how the blood of the sacrifice was sprinkled on the Mercy Seat (*kapporeth*, from *kaphar*) in God's tabernacle. God prophesied that this system would eventually be transferred to His Messiah who would **make His soul an offering for sin** (Isaiah 53:10). This soul offering would satisfy the righteous judgment of God upon the sins of His people (cf. Isaiah 53:11 & John 1:29). This is explained thoroughly in Hebrews 9 as fulfilled in the sacrifice of Jesus Christ. His blood—His body—was sacrificed **once for all** (Hebrews 9:12). Thus, **God set forth** [Jesus] **as a propitiation** [a covering of sin] **by His blood, through faith, to demonstrate His righteousness…** (Romans 3:25).

Biblically defined, propitiation for a follower of Jesus means that His sacrifice was accepted by God on your behalf and, thus, satisfied His judgment on your sins once and for all: **And he Himself** [Jesus] **is the propitiation for our sins; and not for ours only but also for the whole world** (1 John 2:2; cf. 4:10; 1 Tim. 2:6). Jesus, as High Priest, presented His body as a mediatory, reconciliation act, between God and man, and satisfied the penalty for sin for you and anyone else who come to Jesus for the forgiveness of sins.

Another priestly act of Jesus is found in Hebrews 4:13-16, which says, in part, that He **was in all points tempted as we are, yet without sin**; therefore, His followers can come to the throne of God that they **may obtain mercy and find grace to help in time of need**. Jesus demonstrated that, here on earth, a person can avoid succumbing to sins with the help of God's presence. God's grace can replace any sin. Jesus acts as the grace of God. If you have Jesus in you, you have the power to overcome sin in your life (cf. 1 Corinthians 10:13; 1 John 4:4). This is necessary in order for you to act in a priestly role. The priest must first be cleansed of sins.

☞ The Priesthood of Man ☜

In Hebrews 5:5-10, You will discover that, in the flesh, Jesus **offered up prayers and supplications, with vehement cries and tears to Him who was able to save Him from death, and was heard because of His godly fear, though He was a Son, yet He learned obedience by the things which He suffered.** His acts of intense communication with God and the accompanying suffering, due to His obedience, teaches His followers the importance of mediating—praying—in behalf of their fellow man. Becoming **the author of eternal salvation** (5:9) required all the above. For you to continue this priestly function requires the same obedience. If your ministry of reconciliation is going to be effective (accepted), you must imitate this priestly function in behalf of others on this side of eternity.

Notice the importance of this priestly function in Hebrews 7:24-28:

> **But He, because He continues forever, has an unchangeable priesthood. Therefore He is also able to save to the uttermost those who come to God through Him, since He always lives to make intercession for them. For such a High Priest was fitting for us, who is holy, harmless, undefiled, separate from sinners, and has become higher than the heavens; who does not need daily, as those high priests, to offer up sacrifices, first for His own sins and then for the people's, for this He did once for all when He offered up Himself. For the law appoints as high priests men who have weaknesses, but the word of the oath, which came after the law, appoints the Son who has been perfected forever.**

In this passage of Scripture, Jesus is stated as having an eternal, **unchangeable priesthood.** For His followers, this means Jesus is in this priestly function with them forever. This is the **perfected forever** ministry of reconciliation. As a follower of Jesus, you have a sacred and holy function as a priest to mediate on behalf of God and man. You do not become the accepted Sacrifice and you are not the High Priest for man's salvation. But you are the ambassador for that High Priest, and, therefore, the one who explains the way and opens the door of opportunity for a person to become a member of the new commonwealth of God, which is the Bride of Christ. This is an awesome experience in which you, as a priest, have the privilege to participate.

How can this be? Let's read another passage: **...and [He] has made us kings and priests to His God and Father, to Him be glory and dominion forever and ever. Amen** (Revelation 1:6; cf. Revelation 5:9-10; 20:6). This statement is made prior to the future visions of John in the Book of Revelation, and is stated as something that **has** already occurred. You, as a follower of Jesus, are a priest, bringing others to God through the shed blood of Jesus Christ. To do this, you must maintain a holy relationship before God and man. Peter says, **you also, as living stones, are being built up a spiritual house, a holy priesthood, to offer up spiritual sacrifices acceptable to God through Jesus Christ** (1 Peter 2:5). For you, that means you are to be physically pure and morally blameless. You cannot represent God if you yourself are not godly in your behavior and activities. You cannot lead others to Jesus Christ if you yourself are harboring unconfessed sin and need to be led to Him for forgiveness.

The role of a priest requires careful planning and careful administration. A priest could not be a priest by following his own conscience. The ability to perform as a priest is wrapped up in the word, obedience. The First Peter reference bears this out in its context and distinguishes the difference in followers and non-followers of the word of God: **They stumble, being disobedient to the word, to which they also were appointed. But you are a chosen generation, a royal priesthood, a holy nation, His own special people, that you may proclaim the praises of Him who called you out of darkness into His marvelous light;** (vv. 8b-9). You obey because you have been chosen to a priestly function. This places you into **a holy nation** and you are called **His own special people**, a phrase that literally means a special valuable treasure.

ಬ THE PRIESTHOOD OF MAN ೞ

Notice that you are also called into **a royal priesthood**. The word **royal** (*basileion*) means, "that which pertains to a powerful king." This description of your priestly ministry points you to the source of your priesthood. The Almighty God and His Son are using you to present the spiritual kingdom of heaven to those around you and to those with whom you are able to influence. God has set you up as a priest to stand between Him and sinful man by your position in Jesus Christ. In the next chapter, you will discover why your priestly ministry is so important and how to prepare for it.

Transformed!

CHAPTER 10 ~ A Dark River Flows Nearby

In God's earliest covenants with man, nothing was as meticulous as the priestly setup. God had His prophets, His judges, and His kings; but the priesthood of the Levites was set up by Him to be the most difficult—yet rewarding—experience for the Hebrews. The Hebrew people needed a way to communicate with God because of the "darkness" of sin and the power invested in the evil one called, Satan (a.k.a.: the wicked one, or the devil). God set up the priestly system so that man could be delivered from the sinful acts of his fallen human nature and the evil influences of Satan.

In His new covenant, God provided a way out of the darkness: **He has delivered us from the power of darkness and conveyed us into the kingdom of the Son of His love, in whom we have redemption through His blood, the forgiveness of sins** (Colossians 1:12-14). You, as a follower, have been and continue to be **delivered** from a dark power (aorist tense used, which has an undetermined ending). Yet while upon this earth, you are in a vulnerable position with the evil one, who has been given limited permission and power to rule over this darkness. For a person outside the realm of Christ's presence, this power can be terribly strong—even possessive. This is revealed in the word, **delivered**. In Greek, it is *rhuomai*, (from *rheo*, "a current, flow, or force"), which means, "to be rescued or liberated from a strong current or force." It has the idea of someone being dragged or pulled out of impending danger.

In His model prayer, Jesus teaches His followers to pray that God will **deliver** [them] **from the evil one** (Matthew 6:13). In another passage, a priest prophesizes that God would **...grant us that we, being delivered from the hand of our enemies, might serve Him without fear, in holiness and righteousness before Him all the days of our life** (Luke 1:74-75). The Apostle Paul once cried out, **O wretched man that I am! Who will deliver me from this body of death?** (Romans 7:24) All the above verses point to man's need to be delivered from himself, his enemies, and/or the evil one.

The Scriptures prophesy that a **Deliverer will come out of Zion, and He will turn away ungodliness from Jacob; for this is My covenant with them, when I take away their sins** (Romans 11:26b-27). Paul interpreted this Deliverer as the Lord Jesus Christ: **And the Lord will deliver me from every evil work and preserve me for His heavenly kingdom. To Him be glory forever and ever. Amen!** (2 Timothy 4:18) Jesus obtained this power and authority on His cross. It was there that He **disarmed principalities and powers** (Colossians 1:15). Through the blood of Jesus on the cross, every follower can claim victory and power over sin, over death, and over the evil one.

Yet this is where the battle continues between every follower and every non-follower we encounter. Followers of Jesus are to make personal advances in their spiritual growth, and, while advancing, help deliver their fellow man out of the power of darkness:

> **Put on the whole armor of God, that you may be able to stand against the wiles of the devil. For we do not wrestle against flesh and blood, but against principalities, against powers, against the rulers of the darkness of this age, against spiritual hosts of wickedness in the heavenly places. Therefore take up the whole armor of God, that you may be able to withstand in the evil day, and having done all, to stand.** –Ephesians 6:11-13

The above passage in Ephesians speaks primarily to every individual follower of Jesus to be spiritually prepared to do battle

༧ A Dark River Flows Nearby ༨

with the evil one for their own spiritual growth. However, the context is widened a few verses later when Paul asks every armored follower to include him in their prayer battle,
> **that utterance may be given to me, that I may open my mouth boldly to make known the mystery of the gospel, for which I am an ambassador in chains; that I may speak boldly, as I ought to speak.** –Ephesians 6:19-20

As a priest and as an ambassador of Christ, you have been called to **speak** to God (prayer) and to man (proclaim)—that is, to bring the gospel of light into a dark world. You are commissioned to allow the Spirit of the living God to flow through you so that others may be delivered from this darkness and **conveyed into the kingdom of the Son of His love** (Colossians 1:13b). **Conveyed** means to be translated or deported from one place to another. The new place (position) is in Christ and is a position of triumph: **Now thanks be to God who always leads us in triumph in Christ, and through us diffuses the fragrance of His knowledge in every place** (2 Corinthians 2:14). The sweet smell of the knowledge of Christ is to be diffused in every place a follower can touch. Your commission is to bring others into this same sweet smell of Christianity.

The priest and the ambassador are successful when they have performed their duty in such a way that rescues those who are in need of the light of Christ. The darkness is great, but the light is greater. The peril of your position is great, but the triumph is worth it. The triumph is yours to enjoy and yours to spread. So take a stand and prepare yourself in your ministry and position:
> **Stand therefore, having girded your waist with truth, having put on the breastplate of righteousness, and having shod your feet with the preparation of the gospel of peace; above all, taking the shield of faith with which you will be able to quench all the fiery darts of the wicked one. And take the helmet of salvation, and the sword of the Spirit, which is the word of God; praying always with all prayer and supplication in the Spirit, being watchful to this end with all perseverance and supplication for all the saints** (Ephesians 6:14-18).

This is your mediatory role between God and man as a priest and an ambassador.

Ephesians 5:8-21 is just a sampling of many passages that explain your calling and duty as one who has been brought into the glorious light of the gospel of Jesus Christ. This light is to be manifested through you in order to expose **the unfruitful works of darkness** (5:11). You are told to redeem your time (5:16), **understand what the will of the Lord is** (5:17), and **be filled with the Spirit** (5:18). Spiritual transformation occurs in your life so that you might reach the heights of God's purpose for you. From the heights of His purpose you will see the world from a different perspective. You will see man and his darkened predicament as never before. And, best of all, you will be spiritually energized with confidence to fulfill your eternal purpose. Keep flying high, you who follow Jesus Christ, and soar as an eagle into the heavenly places in Christ Jesus our Lord. **But those who wait upon the Lord shall renew their strength; they shall mount up with wings like eagles, they shall run and not be weary, they shall walk and not faint.** –Isaiah 40:31

CHAPTER 11 ~ Possessed

You hear of possession as a negative spiritual experience. There is a demonic possession that is certainly negative; but there is a positive possession when it is attributed to God. Let's read First Peter 2:9 again: **But you are a chosen generation, a royal priesthood, a holy nation, His own special people, that you may proclaim the praises of Him who called you out of darkness into His marvelous light.**

Special people, in Greek, is *laos en peripoiasin*, which literally means, "a people God-encircled, God-possessed." It carries the idea of quality and of preservation. God has chosen you to encircle (possess) you for a purpose: **that you may proclaim the praises of Him.** Before commenting on this, let's verify the possession with additional Scriptures:

...you were sealed with the Holy Spirit of promise, who is the guarantee of our inheritance until the redemption of the purchased possession [*peripoiasin*]**, to the praise of His glory.** –Ephesians 1:13c-14

...to which He called you by our gospel, for the obtaining [*peripoiasin*] **of the glory of our Lord Jesus Christ.** –2 Thessalonians 2:14

...looking for the blessed hope and glorious appearing of our great God and Savior Jesus Christ, who gave Himself for us, that He might redeem us from every lawless deed and

purify for Himself His own special [*periousian*] **people, zealous for good works.** –Titus 2:14

The above verses give a clear description of possession by God in every follower of Jesus. His possession has several purposes. One is to **proclaim** His praises, **to the praise of His glory.** In fact, you see a recurring statement of God's **glory** to be praised or proclaimed. This means that God wants His possession known to the masses by His followers. **Glory** has always pointed to His manifested presence. God wants to be known and reckoned with. He chooses to keep His followers on this earth for the express purpose of revealing Him and His nature. He wants His existence known. If you look carefully at the verses above, you'll notice the Greek word in Titus 2:14 is a little different from the others. This word (*periousian*) comes from the root, *eimi*, which means, "I exist or I am." It not only points to His possession but more pointedly to **His existence in the possession.**

Putting the two words together tells you that God possesses a follower of Jesus in order to expose His existence. In other words, you are a special person—a possessed person—as a follower, **that you may proclaim the praises of Him who called you out of darkness into His marvelous light** (1 Peter 2:9). Underscore **His**. His light is to be proclaimed as holy, as pure, and as morally blameless. You, as the **called...into** [the] **marvelous light** of God, are to be so God-possessed, so God-intoxicated, that people around you see God in and through you.

God-intoxicated?

Have you ever met or dealt with someone who is intoxicated with alcohol or some illegal drug? They act differently don't they? They act as if another spirit has control of them. That's exactly right; another spirit possesses an intoxicated person. Scripture says a follower is not to be intoxicated with wine that lasts for a short time, **but be filled with the Spirit** (Ephesians 5:18); that is, **be continually intoxicated with God.** This is important to understand. If you call yourself a genuine follower of Jesus but another Spirit does not possess you and your nature has not changed, you probably have not received God's nature—you have not become God-possessed, God-intoxicated. If this has not occurred in your conversion, you have missed the whole point of your salvation; you have missed the purpose of God saving you to possess you. You're missing the "joy of the Lord"! (Nehemiah 8:10)

Much of today's Christianity is too sober—that is, too rational and too predictable. Christianity seems to be consumed with competing among the world religions for a socially acceptable standing. Many people around Christians are not aware that God is nearby. In many countries, Christians are beaten, exiled, or killed for their faith. In the more affluent Western countries, many Christians are bent toward acceptance among their peers. Their Christianity is a form of entertainment or a socially acceptable encounter among people. This social form of Christianity has darkened the genuine thing. This so-called Christianity has lost its light and its power. For the most part, God is nowhere close to it. If He were, there would be a noticeable difference between the saved and the lost. The saved follower will be emanating the possessed light of the presence of God's Holy Spirit.

A follower of Jesus is not saved in order to manifest the potential good of man, but to manifest the glorious presence of God. The irony of Christianity is that the follower must continually work to get out of God's way in him. As God's light you're not saved to shine as a person; your light is to shine as God's possession. Use your concordance to chase the word **light** around in the New Testament. Your findings will "illuminate" you! The spiritual light of God—His manifested presence—is what transforms a person. It either saves or sentences; it either brightens or burns; it either draws or destroys. Genuine followers are transformed!

Light

The possession of God in your life produces light. There are two main words for *light* in the New Testament: *phenggos*, which indicates "reflected light" (e.g., the moonlight), and *phos*, which indicates, "manifested light" (e.g., the sunlight). The obvious difference is that one has an inner source of energy (*phos*); the other (*phenggos*) depends on another source of energy shining upon it (reflected light). The following verses of Scripture use *phos* (inner, manifested light) in describing followers of Jesus:

For you were once darkness, but now you are light in the Lord. Walk as children of light. –Ephesians 5:8

You are all sons of light and sons of the day. We are not of the night nor of darkness. –1 Thessalonians 5:5

"While you have the light, believe in the light, that you may become sons of light." These things Jesus spoke... –John 12:36

The nature of God has always been described as **light**. His nature is a consuming light and, therefore, has been a dangerous element to approach. Many times God warned the Hebrews not to approach Him in His manifested light. It would consume their existence (cf. Exodus 19:12-13; Hebrews 12:18-24). Yet, here is Jesus encouraging His followers to **become sons of light**. He is not saying to reflect (*phenggos*) His nature, but to express (*phos*) His nature. All the above-mentioned verses are describing an inner essence, not a reflected experience. While it is possible for followers to experience times of the reflected presence of the Lord, especially in corporate worship, the norm is for His followers to emanate His glorious presence in their daily walk. Let's discover the purpose behind this "normal," day-to-day possession of God's light.

And have no fellowship with the unfruitful works of darkness, but rather expose them. For it is shameful even to speak of those things which are done by them in secret. But all things that are exposed are made manifest by the light, for whatever makes manifest is light. –Ephesians 5:11-13

ಬು POSSESSED ಆ

Followers of Jesus must take a courageous stand and expose **unfruitful works of darkness.** These unfruitful works are described earlier in Ephesians 5 as sexual sins, covetousness, filthiness, foolish talking, coarse jesting, and idolatry (vv. 3-6). The way you expose these is by manifesting the light of Christ that is within you. His presence exposes sin that is contrary to the light of true life. His presence reveals the deadness of darkness. That's why the very next verse says, **Awake, you who sleep, arise from the dead, and Christ will give you light** (*phos*). –Ephesians 5:14

Lazarus—Dead or Alive?

Jesus makes an unusual statement of the light in man in the context of the death of a friend, Lazarus: **Are there not twelve hours in the day? If anyone walks in the day, he does not stumble, because he sees the light of this world. But if one walks in the night, he stumbles, because the light is not in him.** –John 11:9-10

Lazarus was physically dead. You could say his "light" was out. Jesus was about to restore his physical life, showing that He, indeed, was **the resurrection and the life. He who believes in Me, though he may die, he shall live. And whoever lives and believes in Me shall never die. Do you believe this?** (John 11:25-26) Think for a moment: Lazarus was raised to life again, but did Jesus give him a new body? No. In fact, Lazarus came out still in his grave clothes, bound physically. Jesus told those around Lazarus to **loose him, and let him go** (John 11:44). No one is certain what illness put Lazarus in the grave, but it is certain that his death was considered premature. It was equally certain that he would physically die again. Jesus may have turned Lazarus' physical light back on, but Lazarus—like everyone else—would have to do something else to receive the light of spiritual life (John 1:4).

This points, once again, to the emphasis not being on the follower's body. The emphasis should be on what's inside you. Jesus is basically teaching that if you do not have the light of life inside you, then when your **twelve hours in the day**—your life—is over, it's over. When your life is ended, only the spiritual light of Jesus put inside you will stay lit. **Do you believe this?**

ಬ Transformed! ಣ

Followers of Jesus, therefore, are to emanate a living, resurrected spiritual life—this is their light. Every follower's life is to be as miraculous as if he had been physically restored from death. This can only be possible in the manifested presence of the living Jesus Christ. But your "grave clothes" must be removed. This is why you are to walk in a daily fellowship with other followers and in His light: **But if we walk in the light as He is in the light, we have fellowship with one another, and the blood of Jesus Christ His Son cleanses us from all unrighteousness** (1 John 1:7). Verse six says a person who says he is a follower, yet does not walk in His manifested light and is not fellowshipping with other followers, that person is living a spiritual lie and is actually walking in darkness.

Why is much of modern Christianity so ineffective today? Is it not because many so-called "Christians" are dead and walk in darkness? Or, perhaps many are still wearing their grave clothes and need to be loosed. New Testament Christianity—today's guide for genuine Christianity—knows nothing of a weak culture-centered Christianity. Today, many people seek Christianity in order to feel good and to be the recipients of all that its churches and ministers have to offer. They do not want to be bothered about getting involved in the **ministry of reconciliation** or revealing the light of Christ. Yet this "feel good" concept is foreign to New Testament Christianity. The first-century followers of Jesus counted it an honor to suffer for His name. Many modern Christians want to avoid problems and pain. The first-century followers prepared for and expected it, saying that **we must through many tribulations enter the kingdom of God.** –Acts 14:22 (cf., John 16:33; 2 Corinthians 1:4; 1 Thessalonians 3:4)

Why did Jesus say that His followers are to reveal His light? Because He also said that the opposing darkness was nothing short of spiritual death. He wants people of darkness to come to His light in order that they may receive genuine spiritual life. **I am the light of the world. He who follows Me shall not walk in darkness, but have the light of life** (John 8:12). You must ask yourself, "What is my Christianity doing?" Is it shining out the light of life? Are people of darkness around you "seeing" their sins in the light of Christ?

ཉ Possessed ༽

You are the light of the world. A city that is set on a hill cannot be hidden. Nor do they light a lamp and put it under a basket, but on a lampstand, and it gives light to all who are in the house. Let your light so shine before men, that they may see your good works and glorify your Father in heaven.
–Matthew 5:14-16

Jesus gave His followers numerous teachings of the light-life they were to possess: **I must work the works of Him who sent Me while it is day; the night is coming when no one can work. As long as I am in the world, I am the light of the world** (John 9:4-5). Jesus says your light is to bring glory to God in heaven. You are a lighthouse—a spiritual guide for those in the dark storms of life. How many around you are finding the light of life? How many of your family members and friends have slipped into eternity in darkness because you had no spiritual light to offer them? How can your Christianity have no concern or conviction about being the light of life in Christ? There are too many Scriptures to ignore that speak against a life without light as being Christ-like. If Christ is in you, then you must be His light of life. Read John 1:1-9 and note the essence of Jesus' witness. Then ask yourself if this is the essence of your Christian life.

There is nothing more glorious looking than the radiant beauty of a bride as she approaches the altar to join the groom for the vows of matrimony. Therein lies a beautiful picture of light and life. May all genuine followers of Jesus Christ pursue this radiance!

Transformed!

CHAPTER 12 ~ But, What If...?

You have just read the good news of spiritual light. But there is some bad news about being the light of Jesus in this world:
And this is the condemnation, that the light has come into the world, and men loved darkness rather than light, because their deeds were evil. For everyone practicing evil hates the light and does not come to the light, lest his deeds should be exposed. But he who does the truth comes to the light, that his deeds may be clearly seen, that they have been done in God. –John 3:19-21

In the above passage, Jesus is explaining the ongoing battle between evil and good. Let's face it; people who live in darkness have gotten their eyes adjusted so that they are comfortable in their rebellious nature that is against God's holy nature. You have a difficult calling, and that is to bring people into the light of life. Many will not respond to you and many will even hate you for exposing them. They will attack your "holier-than-thou" attitude and tell you it's none of your business what they think or do. But now you know better. Now you know why Jesus Christ is in you. You have no choice in the matter. Light must emanate from you to expose and dispel darkness. This is the nature of the presence of God among mankind. Your life is His now, so set your mind on His nature.

> **If then you were raised with Christ, seek those things which are above, where Christ is, sitting at the right hand of God. Set your mind on things above, not on things on the earth. For you died, and your life is hidden with Christ in God. When Christ who is our life appears, then you also will appear with Him in glory.** –Colossians 3:1-4

The purpose of Christ in you is to condition your mind toward spiritual realities. You are to renew your mind so that you become a spiritual resource for God. This is an eternal partnership that reveals the eternal nature of the Son of God. As you testify to this new partnership nature, you begin to live and act in an eternal way. Why would you want to act otherwise? Read the next passage.

> **And this is the testimony: that God has given us eternal life, and this life is in His Son. He who has the Son has life; he who does not have the Son of God does not have life. These things I have written to you who believe in the name of the Son of God, that you may know that you have eternal life, and that you may continue to believe in the name of the Son of God.** –1 John 5:11-13

Knowing eternal life is in your being gives you great confidence in speaking and living the truth of it. You actually are seated with Christ in His heavenly seat of authority:

> **But God...has made us alive together with Christ...and raised us up together, and made us sit together in the heavenly places in Christ Jesus, that in the ages to come He might show the exceeding riches of His grace in His kindness toward us in Christ Jesus.** –Ephesians 2:4-7

You are light because you are seated with the Light of Life in the **heavenly places**. God set this up so that He might show His love, mercy, and kindness to His followers as well as to those near His followers. Your eternal partnership reveals the true nature of God and the true location of God. Remember, it is **Christ in you**, [that is] **the hope of glory** (Colossians 1:27). And **God willed to make [this] known...among the Gentiles**, that is, the masses of people in darkness. He put this eternal partnership in you. In Christ you have a fellowship that is unique.

ஐ But, What If...? ରଷ

God is faithful, by whom you were called into the fellowship of His Son, Jesus Christ our Lord. –1 Corinthians 1:9

That which we have seen and heard we declare to you, that you also may have fellowship with us; and truly our fellowship is with the Father and with His Son Jesus Christ. –1 John 1:3

Transformed!

CHAPTER 13 ~ Fellowship

That which we have seen and heard we declare to you, that you also may have fellowship with us; and truly our fellowship is with the Father and with His Son Jesus Christ.
—1 John 1:3

Should you feel compelled to **declare** Jesus to others? Isn't witnessing reserved for preachers, evangelists, and those who have that gift of speaking to others? I think the answer is found in the word, **fellowship**. In the Greek language, **fellowship** is *koinonia*, which implies an active, intimate companionship. It means, "to have a participating partnership with someone or something" (social or spiritual intercourse). We get our English word, couch, from *koite*, and, bedroom, from *koiton*. Couch and bedroom are words that imply close companionship and partnership. Even the English word, conception, is associated with this group of Greek words. All these meanings point to the intimate nature of the fellowship being described.

Jesus desires an intimacy with His joint heirs for all eternity. He loves you and He wants you to act on the basis of a loving relationship with Him. Fellowship with Jesus is knowing in your heart that you are one with Him and that you are serving to fulfill His love for you and other followers. In fellowship with Jesus, you will love what He loves. You will aspire to do the things He wants to do. He wants you to **declare** to others your **fellowship** with Him so that they might enjoy a life with Him. He will not leave you alone in your living and testifying here on the earth. You can have great confidence in the fellowship of God's love. His fellowship will fulfill all needs in your inner being. It's like two people getting married and experiencing intimacy together for the first time. This is *koinonia*—an experience of intimacy of which the couple is not ashamed. A couple in love has no problem declaring it and others around them have no problem witnessing the fellowship around this love relationship.

When this type of spiritual fellowship with Jesus and with your fellow believers is demonstrated before others, it will draw them into it as well. You will not have difficulty drawing others into such a love relationship as provided by Jesus Christ. This is a follower's greatest asset in drawing others to Him. Jesus said, **A new commandment I give to you, that you love one another; as I have loved you, that you also love one another. By this all will know that you are My disciples, if you have love for one another** (John 13:35). This spiritual *koinonia* with Jesus will produce spiritual offspring.

Why So Many Divisions?

Sometimes a question or two may surface: *"If this is how genuine followers are to act toward Christ and toward one another, then why can't Christians get along? Why so many different sects of Christianity? Why Baptists, Catholics, or Pentecostals?"*

೮ Fellowship ೮੩

That's a good question and it is an age-old mystery. I think, however, the key to this dilemma may be in the above phrase, **as I have loved you.** Jesus loved in an uncompromising way. He loved best by warning His followers to maintain the truth of the Father and His Word. Jesus did not want another pharisaical group of followers; that is, followers who placed more emphasis on ritual rather than reality, on law rather than love. As Christianity became more acceptable to the masses—especially the governing authorities—the rules for interpreting God's Word became limited to a certain assigned group. Although the beginning of this new era of biblical interpretation may have been intended as harmless and helpful to the masses, it soon became a tool of division. The language of the Bible soon became the language of the clergy and lost touch with the language of the people.

As civilization spread throughout the European continent, the educational advances and diversities of man began to challenge the elite domination of one group of clergy interpreting God's Word. A reformation began to strain the hold of a one-church, one-interpretation mindset. Protesting groups of followers (Protestants) began to form new churches that rallied around a dominant Christian teaching (or teacher). These groups of churches became known as denominations. (This, of course, is my interpretation of Christian history.)

The test of every genuine Christian denomination should be its desire to follow Jesus Christ and His Word to the best of its ability. Genuine Christians should not allow the minor diversities of many denominations to cloud the foundational love of Christ and His Word. There is no pure, infallible church or denomination. Here's a litmus test for yours: if it says and practices that in order for you to be saved, you must somehow get Christ into your life—your inner being—to replace your fallen nature by giving birth to a new spiritual nature, which begins a spiritual transformation in your life, then your church or denomination is going to possess a number of genuine followers of Jesus. However, if replacing your fallen nature with Jesus Christ requires you to do something in order for salvation to occur (e.g., "come to the altar," baptism, money, deeds, a ritual statement or saying, etc.), then it behooves you to investigate the add-on requirement in accordance to the Word of God. Trust only in God's Word to reveal the knowledge and assurance of genuine salvation.

Getting Christ into a man is the cardinal element that connects all genuine Christian denominations to the phrase, **as I have loved you**. How did Jesus love you? He laid down His life, under the authority of the Father, for you. How do you imitate that love? By laying down your life, under the authority of the Father, for Jesus. If your salvation—your conversion—did that, then you have been joined into the love and fellowship—*koinonia*—of the Father and of His Son Jesus Christ (1 John 1:3). Jesus said, **Greater love has no one than this, than to lay down one's life for his friends. You are My friends if you do whatever I command you** (John 15:13-14). Have you laid down all that you are at the feet of His commandments? This is the requirement of God's and Jesus' love and occupation in your life: **If anyone loves Me** [do you?], **he will keep My word** [do you?]; **and My Father will love him, and We will come to him and make our home with him** (John 14:23). This is *koinonia*—this is genuine spiritual fellowship that leads to a transformed life.

CHAPTER 14 ~ Abide in Me

If anyone loves Me, he will keep My word; and My Father will love Him, and We will come to him and make our home with him. –John 14:23

The phrase, **our home**, in John 14:23, needs special attention. The standard King James Bible uses the word **abode**, the same word for **abide** as found in John 15, and the same word for **mansions** in John 14:2. The Greek word for all the above (**our home, abode, mansions**) is *mone*, from *meno* (**abide**). They mean, "to stay (as in a given place), to dwell, to take up residence." It carries the idea of an enduring permanent place.

The love and fellowship of God and Jesus is intended to abide in you for the express purpose of transforming you. Jesus is preparing an eternal place for your new internal being. God has promised an eternal marriage between Jesus and His Bride, the Church. In fact, much of the beauty and grandeur of God's creation is centered on this marriage event that is still future in one sense (that is, when followers' bodies are transformed eternally; cf. 1 Corinthians 15:50-54).

However, Jesus did not say this in the future tense. He did not say He and the Father would come later to make their home with a follower. This statement of Jesus is a present tense reality that you must come to grips with now: Jesus and God set up residence (**abide**) in a person when that person repents of his sin, falls in love with Jesus, and begins to **keep** [His] **word** (John 14:23). The keeping of His word is the betrothal vow between Jesus and the follower. For Jesus and God, love for the follower is defined as abiding in him; for the follower, love for God and Jesus is defined as obeying them. They are both defined and connected in this verse. You cannot separate the two. Note this abiding and obeying connection, as well, in the following verses. In these verses, the *bold italics* identify the connection word in the parenthesis, unless it is obvious:

> And *he who sees Me sees Him who sent Me* (abiding). **I have come as a light into the world, that** *whoever believes in Me* (obeying) **should not abide in darkness.** –John 12:45-46

> **If you love Me,** *keep My commandments* (obeying). **And I will pray the Father, and He will give you another Helper, that He may** *abide with you forever*—**the Spirit of truth...** –John 14:15-17a

> **At that day you will know that** *I am in My Father, and you in Me, and I in you* (abiding). *He who has My commandments and keeps them* (obeying), **it is He who loves Me. And He who loves Me will be loved by My Father, and I will love him and** *manifest Myself to him* (abiding). –John 14:20-21

> *Abide in Me, and I in you.* **As the branch cannot bear fruit of itself, unless it** *abides in the vine*, **neither can you, unless** *you abide in Me*. **I am the vine, you are the branches.** [My Father is the vinedresser (v. 1).] *He who abides in Me, and I in him*, **bears much fruit; for** *without Me you can do nothing* (obeying). –John 15:4-5

> *If you abide in Me, and My words abide in you,* **you will ask what you desire, and it shall be done for you. By this My Father is glorified, that you bear much fruit; so you will be My disciples. As the Father loved Me, I also have loved you;** *abide in My love. If you keep My commandments* (obeying),

❰ Abide in Me ❰

you will abide in My love, just as I have kept My Father's commandments and abide in His love (abiding & obeying). –John 15:7-10

Do not love the world or the things in the world. If anyone loves the world, *the love of the Father is not in Him*...(abiding). **And the world is passing away, and the lust of it; but** *he who does the will of God abides forever* (obeying & abiding). –1 John 2:15, 17

This should be enough to convince you of the inseparable nature you possess with Jesus and God. The wonderful thing about Christianity is the fellowship you can enjoy in the abiding presence of your Lord. This fellowship brings joy and satisfaction in your life. Once the abiding fellowship is experienced, you'll never be satisfied with less. Your life in the light of this love will bring a heavenly atmosphere to earth.

Transformed!

CHAPTER 15 ~ Mission Possible

The tendency of many followers is to sit around and bask in the light of Christ's love. While there are many times when this rightly occurs, the abiding fellowship of Jesus Christ has a further purpose. Let's discover a few facets of that purpose:

Now he who plants and he who waters is one, and each one will receive his own reward according to his own labor. For we are God's fellow workers; you are God's field, you are God's building. –1 Corinthians 3:8-9

We then, as workers together with Him also plead with you not to receive the grace of God in vain. –2 Corinthians 6:1

Paul was the writer to the Corinthian church. He was also a Pharisee before his conversion into Christianity. As a Pharisee, he understood the importance of having a spiritual dwelling place for God. He knew that God had previously instructed the Jews to build Him a dwelling place. This would be the place where God would meet with man. The new covenant also required a spiritual structure in which God would dwell, for man's sake and not His. Man's hands, however, would not make this new structure. God's new and current temple would be in the collective hearts and minds of His people. This was expressed specifically in the prophet Jeremiah's writings (Jeremiah 31:31-34), and was fulfilled in the abiding presence of the Spirit of God:

ೞ Transformed! ෲ

Do you not know that you are the temple of God and that the Spirit of God dwells in you? –1 Corinthians 3:16

And what agreement has the temple of God with idols? For you are the temple of the living God. As God has said: "I will dwell in them and walk among them. I will be their God, and they shall be My people." –2 Corinthians 6:16 (quote collected from Leviticus 26:12, Jeremiah 32:38, & Ezekiel 37:27.)

Like A Rock
For we are God's fellow workers; you are God's field, you are God's building. –1 Corinthians 3:9

The New Testament description of followers as **God's building** is still very applicable to the modern mind. The word, **building**, is *oikodoma*, which comes from *oikos*, meaning *"a dwelling place,"* and *doma*, meaning *"a roof, a dome"* (idea of a protective covering). Together, *oikodoma* means, *"a place of covering, a protective dwelling place."* Paul was teaching that God was using the early followers of Jesus to establish a solid foundation from which a giant Christian empire (a spiritual temple) would be constructed and protected. Jesus is called the **foundation** a few verses later (v. 11). He is also called the **chief cornerstone** in numerous passages (Matthew 21:42; Mark 12:10; Luke 20:17; Acts 4:11; Ephesians 2:20; 1 Peter 2:6-7).

Once Jesus asked His followers, **But who do you say that I am?** (Matthew 16:15) Peter answered correctly saying, **You are the Christ, the Son of the living God** (v. 16). Jesus then blessed him for his response and said, **for flesh and blood has not revealed this to you, but My Father who is in heaven. And I also say to you that you are Peter, and on this rock I will build My church, and the gates of Hades** [hell] **shall not prevail against it** (v. 17b-18).

The word, **rock**, in this passage has always been an issue of debate between the Catholics and the Protestants (non-Catholics). The Catholic Church has always stood behind the dogma that Jesus was pointing or referring to Peter when he said His church would be built upon this **rock**. The non-Catholics, however, point to the change of the word tense used for **rock** when Jesus made this church-building reference. Let's dissect the words a bit.

First of all, the word for **Peter** is *petros*, which means, *"a (piece of) rock."* It is larger than a stone (*lithos*) but smaller than *petra*, the word used for **rock** that Jesus refers to that would be the foundation on which He would build His church. The context of the statement leans more to the reference of rock (*petra*) as being either Jesus himself, His or Peter's statement, or to the group of disciples. It doesn't seem to fit the immediate context for Jesus to place such a high blessing on Peter, then, in the same breath, use the more generic massive word for **rock** (*petra*) than **Peter** (*petros*) to address him. If the statement was to be a major directive to the church, or to Peter, Jesus should have been more careful in His use of words. If, however, He pointed to Himself, or to the group of disciples, or to either statement, then the word change fits perfectly. The larger context, which features several incidences with Peter (Matthew 16:21-23; 17:1-5), seems to downplay any special privileges addressed to him.

The Rock of the church is Jesus Christ, for He alone is called the Chief Cornerstone (1 Peter 2:6; Ephesians 2:20). He is the foundation upon which the church is built. His early followers, who were called **apostles** (Ephesians 2:20), joined the Hebrew prophets in introducing and building God's spiritual **temple** (v. 21). From there the building expands to include all followers of Jesus Christ, **in whom the whole building, being fitted together, grows into a holy temple in the Lord, in whom you also are being built together for a dwelling place of God in the Spirit** (v. 21-22). Followers of Jesus are called **living stones** (*lithos*) that **are being built up a spiritual house, a holy priesthood, to offer up spiritual sacrifices acceptable to God through Jesus Christ.** –1 Peter 2:5

ಬ TRANSFORMED! ಲ

Think about this whole idea of a spiritual **holy temple**. If it's going to be **acceptable to God**, if it's going to be **holy**, it must be without spot or blemish. How can you, as a follower of Jesus, fit into such a design? It can only be answered with a belief in the follower's possession of the Holy Spirit. You, as a follower of Jesus Christ have been possessed by God's Spirit and have been declared righteous so that you may join the throng of followers throughout the ages into this holy place for God to occupy. And it's as solid as the Rock of Jesus. Do not doubt your inner spiritual strength and being. Though the **outward man is perishing, yet the inward man is being renewed day by day** (2 Corinthians 4:16). Your daily renewal places you into a usable position with God. And His temple has an important function. Let's look into this a bit further.

God's temple has always been seen as a place where God meets with man. Within His temple, there were a number of instruments used to make man's encounter with God an acceptable and redeeming event. As spiritual instruments of God, every follower has a functioning role of bringing people into an encounter with God through His accepted, eternal sacrifice Jesus Christ. But how do you do this? The ways to introduce Jesus to others are many. In one Scripture followers are called an **epistle of Christ** (2 Corinthians 3:3). This means you should stand up and let people "read" the message of your Christian life. Other Scriptures say followers are **ministers** (servants—*diakonos*) of the **new covenant** and of **God** (2 Corinthians 3:6; 6:4). This means you are to serve the message of the new covenant of God to others. *Diakonos* are people who go to others and offer practical service to them. Still, another Scripture says followers are **ambassadors for Christ** with a **ministry of reconciliation** (2 Corinthians 5:17-20). This means you have been given a supreme authoritative role of representing Christ to man. As His ambassador, you are negotiating, with man, God's "terms of peace."

This is your mission and the ongoing mission of Jesus Christ until He returns. **The Lord...is not willing that any should perish but that all should come to repentance. But the day of the Lord will come as a thief in the night...** (2 Peter 3:9-10a). Your Lord has declared the

☙ Mission Possible ❧

mission. You have been gifted to do the good work you were created for (Ephesians 2:10). You have the abiding presence of the Holy Spirit to empower you in the conflict of spirit-versus-flesh (soul). As you express your gift(s) to those around you, the rewards will be yours to receive in the presence of Almighty God. Show your love by obeying His word, thus fulfilling your purpose in life.

I must work the works of Him who sent Me while it is still day; the night is coming when no one can work. As long as I am in the world, I am the light of the world. –Jesus, in John 9:4-5

Therefore we make it our aim, whether present or absent, to be well pleasing to Him. For we must all appear before the judgment seat of Christ, that each one may receive the things done in the body, according to what he has done, whether good or bad. –2 Corinthians 5:9-10

Transformed!

CHAPTER 16 ~ Circumcision – 'A Sign of the Covenant'

To the modern reader in the Western culture, the subject of physical circumcision is a private matter, rarely discussed even among men. Circumcision is performed today primarily as a hygienic procedure on males soon after they are born. It is still performed among Jewish (and other Middle Eastern) families as a religious rite when a male child reaches a certain age; however, many people fail to comprehend the rich spiritual symbolism behind circumcision and why God chose it to permanently mark His people.

Circumcision was not a secret rite; it was prominent throughout the Bible. The first mention of circumcision in the Bible is found in Genesis 17:10-14 and is in the context of a covenant agreement between God and Abraham. It reads in part:

> **This is My covenant which you shall keep, between Me and you and your descendants after you: Every male child among you shall be circumcised; and you shall be circumcised in the flesh of your foreskins, and it shall be *a sign of the covenant* between Me and you...and My covenant shall be in your flesh for an everlasting covenant** (v. 10-11, 13b; emphasis added).

The **everlasting covenant** being referred to is God's promise of descendants from Abraham and Sarah (Genesis 15:12-21). So, it is fitting that the **flesh of your foreskins** became the physical sign of God's covenant for Abraham's descendants. From Abraham on, every Jewish male was to be circumcised as the mark of a man in covenant with God. Even non-Jewish men, who wanted to participate in the worship of God and in the festivities of the Jews, had to be circumcised (cf., Exodus 12:43-48).

In time, circumcision became more than the sign of a covenant relationship with God. Along with the covenant came the understanding that the blood of circumcision and the removal of the flesh became symbolic of the removal of sin from the heart (Colossians 2:11). No man could covenant with God unless there was a blood sacrifice offered for sin. The foreskin of a male was the blood sacrifice that allowed him to covenant with God. This was the requirement provided by God. This act provided an approachable relationship between God, a man, and a man's family.

The covenant of circumcision can be symbolically explained in the flesh from at least four perspectives: it is the covenant of permanency, the covenant of intimacy, the covenant of ancestry, and the covenant of humility.

The Covenant of Permanency

God told Abraham, **I will establish My covenant between Me and you and your descendants in their generations, for an everlasting covenant...** (Genesis 17:7). The sign of the everlasting covenant would be circumcision. Circumcision would be that permanent mark on every male who was in covenant with God. **Once circumcised, always circumcised**; there could be no revocation of the physical sign.

God intended for a man in covenant with Him to be permanently marked as a proof of his relationship. Circumcision was no minor afterthought; it was a family matter that would allow a man and his family to continue a marked line of Abrahamic descendants and to maintain a relationship with God (cf. Exodus 4:24-26).

ಐ Circumcision – 'A Sign of the Covenant' ଔ

The Covenant of Intimacy

From a physical perspective, circumcision may be realized in times of intimacy with a spouse. The two would become one. As such, a male's circumcision allowed him to be as pure as possible each time he entered a bonding relationship with his spouse. Thus, circumcision would allow two people to experience intimacy in its purest form.

This is the desire of God with man—an intimate experience of relationship in its purest form. God's holiness interacts within man's innermost part—his heart. In intimacy, God purifies man's relationship with Him. Thus man must undergo the circumcision of his heart (Romans 2:28-29). The "foreskin" of sin must be removed from his heart before man can have an intimate relationship with God. Once sin is removed, intimacy with God is unhampered and unlimited.

The Covenant of Ancestry

Circumcision is also the covenant of ancestry. It is from a man's body that the lineage of his descendants would be determined. God chose circumcision to remind the man of his responsibility to keep his descendants in covenant with God.

God has designed His intimacy with man so that every follower of Jesus who has an intimate relationship with God will produce spiritual offspring—descendants. As Spirit joins with spirit in Christ, new followers will be born. This is the design and nature of God—**intimacy produces ancestry**. God's promise of descendants to Abraham was to be miraculous, but He still used the physical part of intimacy for the miraculous to occur. For you and me to experience the satisfaction of spiritual offspring, we must still interact with people. We must reveal (explain) our relationship—our covenant—with God in such a way that others will want the same experience.

The Covenant of Humility

Circumcision is also the covenant of humility. No place on a man is more vulnerable—more sensitive—than where circumcision occurs. To mark a covenant with God at that physical location is to place man under a humble position before God and before other men as a proof of his covenant with God. Someone else usually performs circumcision on a male when the male is very young. Later on in life, the mark of circumcision would remind the male that someone else was involved in the way he would experience intimacy. It is indeed a humbling thought.

God wants all followers of Jesus to know that if they will humble themselves before Him, He will exalt them in due time (1 Peter 5:6). Spiritual offspring will surely come as God decrees it and man will be exalted as he gives God the glory and honor for such an experience of intimacy.

Spiritual Circumcision

The above four perspectives of circumcision give you a better understanding of a follower's relationship with Jesus. Paul writes that all followers of Jesus **were also circumcised with the circumcision made without hands, by putting off the body of the sins of the flesh, by the circumcision of Christ** (Colossians 2:11). The cutting of the body of Jesus on His cross—His bodily sacrifice—was the circumcision that removed the **body of the sins of the flesh. For [God] made Him who knew no sin to be sin for us, that we might become the righteousness of God in Him.** –2 Corinthians 5:21

For spiritual circumcision to become a reality between God and man (speaking generically here), He had to cut away and remove forever man's sin. Sin was man's curse for his rebellion—his divorce—against God. **Cursed is everyone who hangs on a tree** (Galatians 3:13; Deuteronomy 21:23). Jesus accepted His role as the curse for sin in order to provide man a new intimate relationship with the Father. All man would have to do is come to God through this **blessing** and **receive the promise of the Spirit through faith** (Galatians 3:14). In the New Covenant, physical circumcision was

ಲ Circumcision – 'A Sign of the Covenant' ಣ

replaced with baptism as a sign of a man's covenant with God (Colossians 2:11-12).

The Bride of Christ is the Church. Jesus wants intimacy with His bride. He wants descendants through His bride. He wants His bride to humble herself before Him: a sign of respect, a sign of love, and a sign of obedience. This can only happen when each member of the Church is marked with the circumcision of his heart in the Spirit (cf. Romans 2:25-29). This reunites God's love with his creature of love (man) and thus creates true spiritual intimacy.

Are you experiencing spiritual intimacies with God? Not sure? Are you displaying physical fruit of the Spirit? To help you through this, think of all the physical displays of a bride. She plans for the encounter. She is adorned in her finest. She is radiant, vibrant, and excited. She is clean and pure. She is beautiful in the eyes of her beloved. She is surrendering her authority to her husband. She is relocating her place of residence. She is taking on a new name. She is revealing and presenting all that she is and has to her husband. She is becoming vulnerable in her union to him. She is making her body available for offspring. When conception occurs, she is changed forever. She accepts a new role and responsibility toward those around her, especially her offspring.

Again I ask: Have spiritual intimacies occurred in your relationship with Christ? Does the bride in the above paragraph describe you? Does an intimate relationship with Christ permanently mark you as a Christian, or is your relationship with Him self-centered instead of God-centered? What I see and hear about many a person's Christianity is their happiness about going to heaven or getting their sins forgiven. These are certainly some of the benefits of genuine conversion into Christianity. But to make this your focus is like being happy and content in a physical marriage because your spouse has promised you happiness, a new home, and plenty of money **after your spouse dies**. Is that the most important thing in a physical marriage? Is that why a couple gets married? I don't think so.

God wants an intimate **relationship** with you now. That's spelled: R-E-L-A-T-I-O-N-S-H-I-P—not R-E-L-I-G-I-O-N. He already had the best and most productive religion on earth in Judaism. But Judaism, at its best, was incapable of keeping a follower in a genuine intimate relationship with God. God wants intimacy with you and this is the essence of His being (or Being) in you. If you receive nothing else from this book, please let this section dive into your innermost self. **Genuine followers of Jesus Christ are betrothed to Him in a marriage covenant.** They have received the redemptive promise of matrimony and are committed to Him for an intimate relationship for all eternity.

Universally, all believers comprise the Bride of Christ—the Church. Read Ephesians 5:22-33 again. Read Revelation 21:9-27 again. What do these passages say to you about a relationship with Christ? Why settle for anything less?

Spiritual transformation is the process every follower must yield to in his inner spirit in order for genuine spiritual intimacies to occur between God and man. As this book concludes, my prayer is for you to go further with God in the unique relationship He has provided for His followers. Allow His intimacy to flood your heart. Feel the warmth of His nearness. Experience the results of His intimacy as you see others around you become spiritually **born again** into this same relationship you experience with your Creator God—your Heavenly Father—and the Lord Jesus Christ. Nurture your spiritual offspring as they experience the Spirit of the Living God setting up residence in them forever and ever. This is your calling and this is the natural result of your relationship with God as **spiritual transformation, the power of knowing God**, occurs in your innermost being. Obey your calling and experience the results of genuine Christianity.

The grace of the Lord Jesus Christ, and the love of God, and the communion [*koinonia*—intimacy] **of the Holy Spirit be with you all. Amen.** –2 Corinthians 13:14

Postscript

We are told that love is of God; **and everyone who loves is born of God and knows God...for God is love** (1 John 4:7b, 8b.). Anyone who claims to be a Christian should be naturally drawn into a special, personal relationship with Jesus Christ.

What I have written in this book may seem foreign to some Christians, but it shouldn't. We speak often of a "personal relationship" with Christ; yet we stop short of describing that personal relationship as a time of intimate fellowship (*koinonia*) with Him.

My prayer throughout this writing has been that the reader will be drawn closer to our great God and Savior, Jesus Christ. If it has, then to God be the glory for the great things He continues to do.

Find His love and pursue it. Embrace His love and live in it. Then you can confidently express His love to all others. This is the commandment of Christ that reveals the glory of the oneness of His and the Father's love in us:

I in them, and You in Me; that they may be made perfect in one, and that the world may know that You have sent Me, and have loved them as You have loved Me. – John 17:23

May our Lord's love and grace be upon you. – JRJ

A Closing Word

If you have found some portion of this work to have been of benefit to you, would you please consider doing a favor for this author?
- Pray for his ministry of speaking and writing.
- Pray for ways to spread this work to others. Perhaps you have family or friends you can encourage by purchasing them a copy. This work is especially useful to introduce someone to the wonderful life of Christ-likeness. This work may become a special life-changing gift for someone.
- Pray for ways this author may speak at your fellowship of believers—a church, Bible study group, or similar gathering.
- A small paragraph from you on how this work benefited you may become helpful as an entry on future printings (*What Others Are Saying About This Book*). Please email me.

Thank you for your part in my ministry.

jj@HisAboundingGrace.org
www.HisAboundingGrace.org

߷ Transformed! ☙

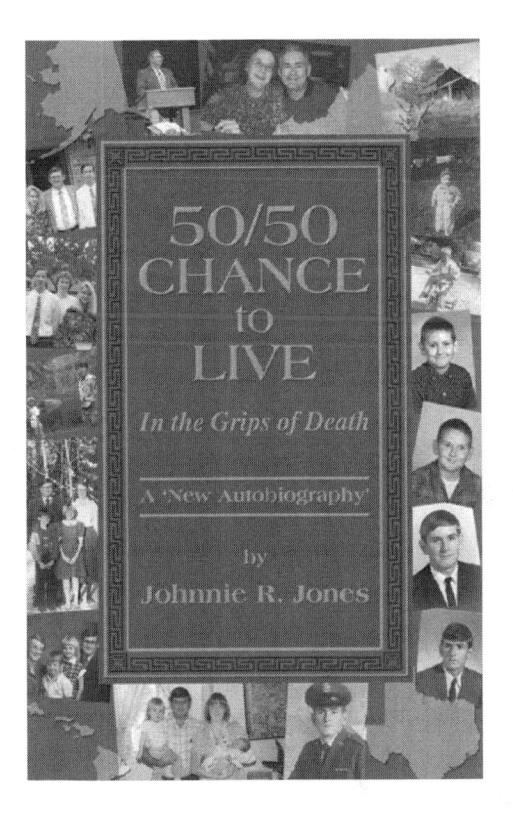

© 2009; 330 pages
From Virginia to Texas, to Hawaii and Alaska, follow the tracks of one man's trail that slipped through the grips of death five times, while touching the lives of thousands. Order online at: www.HisAboundingGrace.org

"Here is the story of a man and his family who have walked through difficulties as severe as anyone can face..." –Dr. Paige Patterson, President, Southwestern Baptist Theological Seminary

"...an outstanding journal of one man's triumph over seemingly impossible circumstances. It is a must read!" –Dr. Jimmy Draper, President Emeritus, LifeWay Christian Resources

Transformed!